Creating a Garden for the Senses

Creating a Garden

TEXT BY JEFF COX

for the Senses

PHOTOGRAPHS BY JERRY PAVIA

Abbeville Press Publishers • New York • London • Paris

Editor: Susan Costello
Designer: Charles Davey
Production Editor: Alice Gray
Production Manager: Simone René

First edition, second printing

Library of Congress Cataloging-in-Publication Data
Cox, Jeff, 1940-
Creating a garden for the senses / text by Jeff Cox: photographs by Jerry Pavia.
        p. cm.
Includes index.
ISBN 1-55859-329-2
1. Gardens—Design. 2. Senses and sensation. 3. Gardens—Pictorial Works. I. Pavia, Jerry. II. Title
SB473.C686 1993
712'.2—dc20
                    93-3281

                CIP

Photographer's Acknowledgments

In addition to all the gardens, gardeners, and garden designers already mentioned in the captions, I would like to give special thanks to the following people for the time and energy they gave to me to make this the best book that it could be. In France: Madame Andlau; Prince Wolkonsky; Didier Willery; Georges Leveque; Michel Lamontagne; Madame Kargere; Madame Lindsay at Giverny; Tiba. In England: Sally Wood and the entire staff of the Garden Picture Library; Ron Sutherland; Rosemary Verey; John Brookes; Christopher Lloyd. In America: Mary Smith; Connie Cross; Pam Lord; Lois Woodall; Norman Johnson; Allen Rokach; Cindy White; Anne Schwartz; Ryan Gainey; Marco Polo Stephano; Lynden Miller; Wirsche Photo Lab of Spokane, Washington; United Airlines. Finally, I'd like to thank my friend, Will Venard, for his part in our conversations over the years about art, spirituality, baseball, and anything else that came up in our talks. His thoughts have helped the creative part of my being to surface and express itself.

Author's Dedication

For Susanna
—JEFF COX

Photographer's Dedication

For my parents, Charles and Gladys Pavia of Utica, New York
—JERRY PAVIA

PAGE 1 AND 160. *If the entrance to one's heart could take physical form, it would look like these Sweetheart roses (Rosa 'Cecile Brunner') growing over the gate to Jody Honnen's garden in Rancho Santa Fe, California. One reason this scene is so effective is because it uses just a few stunning elements to produce a lush sensuousity.*

PAGES 2-3. *The refined aesthetic of a Japanese garden appeals to many people's sense of beauty. In recent years, gardeners in the Pacific Northwest have borrowed much inspiration from this source. At the Nitobe Japanese Garden in Vancouver, British Columbia, a footbridge and flowering pink cherries (Prunus) are reflected in the water.*

PAGE 5. *One reason rock gardens are so enticing is that there is an intriguing sensuousity about the hard, colorless, and permanent rocks mingled with the soft, colorful, and evanescent mounds of flowers.*

PAGES 6-7. *Here's a subtle touch: the sinuous line of the grass path at the garden of Princess Sturdza at La Vasterival in Varengeville-sur-mer in France is repeated in the farthest right trunk of the group of three. The pruning scar on that trunk shows that someone along the way took off a limb. By visualizing the limb in place, we can see that it would have interrupted and concealed the artful interplay of these lines.*

Contents

Introduction

GARDENS WHERE THE SENSES BLOOM

ABOVE. *Love, desire, passion—these are required of the gardener, and of the garden. Here a cool September rain has drenched these lovesick Michaelmas daisies (*Aster *'Harrington's Pink').*

LEFT. *Touch in a garden may involve wildlife visitors. Here a monarch butterfly ever-so-gracefully touches down on a butterfly bush (*Buddleia davidii*) at the Barry Ferguson Garden in Oyster Bay, New York.*

PAGES 8-9. *A carpet of soft, feathery horsetail (*Equisetum*) washes around rough tree trunks, inviting the touch of visitors in the Botanic Garden of the University of California at Berkeley.*

No place on earth is more sensuous than a garden. In its sights, sounds, tastes, touches, and smells, we find home and heart and love. The purpose of this book is to help us all—gardeners and garden lovers—more deeply appreciate the sensuous and sensual qualities of plants. Our appreciation will enrich the time we spend outdoors and enhance our pleasure in our gardens.

Sensuous and *sensual*—these words need defining at the outset. According to *Webster's Third New International Dictionary,* "Sensual implies gratification . . . the indulgence of appetite. Sensuous can imply less an indulgence of appetite than an aesthetic gratification or delight, as in beauty of color, sound, or artistic form." This book considers both the sensuous and sensual aspects of plants.

Such a project may sound reductionist. Instead of relaxing and enjoying the garden as a whole, must we separate it into its visual, aural, olfactory, tactile, and gustatory elements? Aren't we killing the unicorn by doing this?

No. The deeper our understanding of the sensible qualities of plants, the richer our experience of the whole garden will be. A neophyte can hear Beethoven's Ninth Symphony and enjoy it, but a person with musical training understands it in a deeper way. In the garden, too, subtext enriches text. Often we are not consciously aware of how our senses perceive plants. This book is intended to bring these unconscious sensory experiences into the bright light of full consciousness. In fact, when we again see the garden at night, the darkness will have meaning and presence.

This book is designed to inspire the natural creativity in every gardener and to suggest ideas for great gardens everywhere. A gardener who more fully understands plants and our sensory responses to them can be a more effective designer. Once we become aware of the different sensory elements a garden contains, our design intentions gain more content. We find meaning in the placement of plants, and we become more careful in our decisions. For example, the rose 'Gruss an Aachen' carries a fruity (even tutti-frutti) fragrance. If we use not just color but fragrance in making decisions, we may discover that the clove scents of spicebush viburnums or carnations combine well with that fruity note and not so well with the perfumy fragrance of damask roses.

One of the best ways to unleash your own creativity is to look at what other successful gardeners have wrought. Photographer Jerry Pavia's photographs provide examples of the techniques and themes under discussion. To assemble his photographs, Pavia traveled through the United States and Europe seeking out the sort of beauty that touches the senses and, through them, the heart.

As the photos amply show, no garden is wholly man-made. Rather, it is the joint product of the person who arranges it, the plants that clothe it, the tendencies and forces of the earth and stones from which it arises, and the impetuous nature that drives it all forward. The gardener plants the shrub, but the plant finds the light and displays its blossoms according to its own rules. Balance is the key word in most of the ways we design gardens: balanced color, texture, value, form, and visual weight. Well-balanced gardens have a quality of restfulness and exquisite perfection, with plants chosen and placed like words in a perfect poem.

When all the plants are planted, and the gardener has retired, nature comes in and puts on the finishing touches. A cardinal flower may volunteer to mark a field of blue with an accent of crimson. Or a clump of spiky, upright grasses may arise, in seeming answer to the pendulous limbs of a weeping cherry.

Nature can change the mood of a garden completely in just minutes. A sunny, cheery garden turns somber as gray clouds darken the sky. Tall junipers sweep back and forth in the wind and rain, scrubbing the sky clean.

The cold of winter can bring on a deathlike state, plunging ice daggers into tender foliage and soft earth. All the busy green of summer vanishes like a dream. Life retracts into roots that become hidden and forgotten in the frozen soil.

Nature operates the infinite interworkings of biological mechanisms in myriad forms, from gigantic to miniscule, intricate to simple, delicate to sturdy. And all of it is shot through with awareness.

Awareness requires sense organs. It is through the senses that all creatures—animal or vegetable—experience the world. Because every creature's sensory equipment differs, each experiences a different world. Within each of these worlds is the opportunity for a creature to make its way and survive, but for that to happen, it must do what it is driven to do, programmed to do—you might almost say, what it loves to do. The mole loves to chew the succulent worm. The hawk loves to swoop to pluck a sparrow from the air, just as the earthworm loves to burrow through topsoil. A plant's leaves turn to catch the beloved sun.

Love, desire, passion—these are all words that we can use to describe the organizing principles and the driving forces behind nature's purposes. When we look at a garden, we are looking at the total of many purposes, the passions of many forms of life. Plants directly display their organizing principles in their forms, but animals do so by their demeanor. Thus it is with passion that we need to approach the sensuous garden and to appreciate its fullness.

Can you remember a sunny afternoon when, as a small child, you wandered down a path into a low part of a yard or field, where wet

OPPOSITE TOP. *Little violas known as Johnny-jump-ups greet our passing gaze with their cheery hellos.*

OPPOSITE BOTTOM. *For visual appeal, few plants match the adorable little white bells of* Campanula formanekiana, *here tumbling from a wall at the Royal Botanic Garden of Edinburgh, Scotland.*

RIGHT. *All the senses seem caught up by this scene at the Beth Chatto Gardens, Elmstead Market, Colchester, England. The smell of the plants. The taste, touch, and sound of the water. The sight of the artful landscaping and the flower colors. Together they make a sensuous place, perhaps one to hide in.*

ABOVE. *Our cares are washed away by the wisteria's fragrant, lavender rain. This place of protective refuge, in the Severence Garden in Seattle, Washington, appeals to human instincts passed down to us by our prehuman ancestors.*

RIGHT. *One can just see them running, laughing, flirting —he in doublet and buskin, she in gown and wimple, love abloom along with pink geraniums. This romantic setting is found at the Acorn Bank Garden at Temple Sowerby, Penrith, England.*

PAGES 16-17. *Our sense of sight is mightily entertained by this curdled topiary at the Woodland Rose Garden in Seattle, Washington. Its severe form is balanced by the loose, spreading crown of the tree at the right. Roses dance merrily on their bushes in the foreground to complete the show.*

grasses grew high, and where the path was a muddy puddle? Remember putting your hands into that mud, all warm and wet from the sun? Remember the smell of the mud and the grass? And the wetness seeping through your clothes as you got deeper into the joys of the puddle? There might have been a butterfly or a frog in the tall grass, or a tiny glittering golden fly, all in beautiful colors. Remember how the warm grasses and weeds hummed with the sounds of insects?

To fully experience the garden, we have to experience it as a child might: sensuously, not just as a prettty picture arrayed for our visual enjoyment. Full enjoyment involves feeling the earth, and the weight of stones, and seeing beauty in decay, and smelling the freshly made compost. It comes to us through the delights of the eye, the sound of the wind, the touch of the grass, the taste of the berry, and the scent of the rose.

One by one our senses are captivated and charmed by the garden, and then all together: We are swimming in birdsong and perfume, fresh flavor and cool touches, all decorated with gorgeous colors.

The garden invites us to lie down on the grass and feel the sun and the wind and the earth. The rose invites us with its scent. The flash of a silver-sided fish invites us to peer more deeply into the lily pond. Clusters of ripe raspberries invite us to savor their taste.

As we enjoy the garden and love what it offers us, we draw close to nature and her ways. We are on the right path. The garden is telling us

about ourselves, and, even more deeply, about how one of its purposes is to care for us—its human gardeners and visitors.

If you have ever created a garden and had a love for it, you will know this to be true. The garden soothes us and delights us, and we find healing care there, too. These gifts are given unfailingly, like a mother's love. The garden is a love song, a duet between a human being and "mother" nature. Gardeners do surely come to love their plants. They love the glimpses of natural orderliness that shine through the chaos of sheer growth. And they love the beauty that abounds there, both planned and found. In return, nature responds in kind to love and care.

We can feel this even when the garden is not ours. Ah, but when it is! Then we are not just listening to the duet, but singing in it. We find sites for our plants that we think they will like, and if we succeed, the plants respond with healthy, beautiful growth. We dig the soil, and the radishes grow big and sweet. We arrange the stones, and the moss fills in the spaces with its green bass tones. We are paid for our work with the coin of beauty that astonishes all our senses.

The Sensuous Garden

Who comes calling us softly to life
*   through the soft spring rain,*
Shouting bright colors back
*   at the strong summer sun?*
Who withers in the autumn's ruinous
*   rain,*
And ceases even to whisper
*   when the snow cover comes?*

Eyes open slowly
*   to the bramble's spare beauty.*
It may take a lifetime, an eon, or
*   more.*
Any tongue can taste sugar
But few can taste pleasure—
The fruits of hard years
*   growing sweet in the sun.*
Thorns and scratches
*   make the way welcome*
For cool, silky grasses.

The vast, airy sky seems so empty—
How long 'til we hear
*   its traces of song,*
And catch the sweet scent
*   of a heavenly fragrance*
From a tree that is blooming
*   beyond the beyond?*

—JEFF COX

Sight

Almost any garden, if you see it at just the
right moment, can be confused with Paradise.
Henry Mitchell

It is always properly humbling to realize that our vision, while it seems entirely complete to us, encompasses only a narrow segment of the whole electromagnetic spectrum. If we could see the whole spectrum, we would be able to "see" our plants by radio and television waves, by telephone telemetry, by the waves from microwave transmitters and ovens, by ultraviolet light and infrared heat waves, in the pointillistic dance of cosmic rays, and by the universal shine of gamma rays born in the cores of collapsed stars.

Certain animals can see by some of these invisible lights. Bees, for instance, can see ultraviolet light. When we look at flower petals under ultraviolet light, the hidden patterns and shapes that guide bees to the nectaries become apparent.

What would we see if we saw by the whole spectrum? No one knows, but this is sure: There is more to the picture than meets the eye. What we actually see is a function of being human. Our eyes operate only in the wavelengths we call visible light. In understanding a garden, it helps to remember that the scenery is the human visual "take"; there is much more to the thing itself.

Sight is the chief sense for perceiving an ornamental garden and deserves first consideration. Earth, rocks, water, buildings, foliage, wood, and flowers form the scenery, but we judge their beauty in terms of color, form, mass, texture, composition, scale, and balance. Our ocular vision is only a part of our visual sense, however. The inner visions of imagination and insight, although they are not based on the ability to perceive visible light, also come into play. To judge formal artistic qualities, we measure what we see in reality against an internal ideal of pure beauty. Our eyes are the sense organs that bring us the picture, but it is inside, in our minds, that we feel emotionally moved by beauty—or not, depending on the garden.

ABOVE. *Garden scenes can allude to other sights we have seen. A flock of elegant magnolia blossoms (*Magnolia quinquepeta 'Nigra'*) settles like birds on the branches above a tossing sea of* Rodgersia podophylla. *The photo was taken at Sissinghurst, England.*

OPPOSITE. *The shape of the monolith in the water is reflected by a tall, conical juniper in this springtime scene at the Japanese Garden on the grounds of the Washington Park Arboretum in Seattle, Washington. Note the sparing, subtle, and elegant use of color.*

PAGES 18-19. *Gardens represent our attempts to bring our inner ideals of beauty to physical reality. It is a lovely dream indeed that has come to life in Prince Wolkonsky's garden in Tredarzac, France.*

THE NATURE OF BEAUTY AND THE BEAUTY OF NATURE

What is the inner ideal of beauty? Where does it come from? Children seem to come into this world with an aesthetic sense already in place, although this sense certainly can develop and mature over time. While a child may think that Disneyland is beautiful, the adult probably prefers Fallingwater or Saint Paul's Cathedral.

Scientists have found that human beings prefer certain kinds of landscapes over others, and they theorize that this phenomenon shows our species' link to our ancestral home—the grasslands of Africa. When shown photographs of several landscapes and asked to choose which they preferred, people everywhere—even those from tropical forests who had never been in grasslands in their lives—tended to choose grass landscapes. Maybe this inborn aesthetic sense explains our culture's fascination with the lawn. Subjects in scientific tests of landscape preference also show a strong preference for water—which may be why most parks have lots of lawn and water.

People like landscapes they find legible—that is, with features that allow for easy orientation. One of the most legible landscapes in the United States is the Yosemite Valley, because it has a number of unmistakable features: El Capitán, Bridal Veil Falls, Cathedral Rocks, Yosemite Falls, North Dome, and

Half Dome. One or more of these landmarks can always be seen from anyplace in the valley. It is just about impossible to get lost in Yosemite.

Scientists have also found that people have an innate preference for places where one can see over long distances and refuges where they can take shelter and hide unseen.

Rob Thayer, of the Department of Environmental Design at the University of California at Davis, realized that he was in such a preferred spot when wandering in the Los Padres National Forest in southern California. "I saw a depression in one of the rocks, and knew that here

OPPOSITE. *Sometimes the inner conception is formal, as along this walkway at the Garden at Elk Rock in Portland, Oregon, where an ornamental witch hazel (*Hamamelis x intermedia *'Ruby Glow') hoists the flame of conservativism behind severely clipped boxwood hedges.*

TOP. *The masterfully composed garden of Jim and Connie Cross in Cutchogue, New York, explodes in a spectacular display of effects for the visual sense: ornamental foxtails (*Pennisetum alopecuroides*) arch softly, low-growing Colorado blue spruce (*Picea pungens*) bristles,* Verbena Canadensis *splashes the bottom of the scene with its soft pink flowers, and as we work back into the picture, we find cool water, hot sunlight, rough rocks, and many kinds and colors of foliage.*

RIGHT. *A Japanese garden may be even more beautiful in fall than in spring, as shown by the orange-russet leaves of the Japanese maple (*Acer palmatum*) at the Portland Japanese Garden in Oregon. The placement of the stones, bowl, and bamboo waterspout are traditional elements of a Japanese garden, whose design can be as formal in its natural way as a tea ceremony.*

was where the Indian women once ground their acorns. Looking around, I knew why: it was a delightful spot sheltered by trees, with water nearby, where anyone would feel at home."

Besides our innate human preferences for certain landscape features, we also develop a set of personal preferences over time that reflect our experiences and the content of our hearts. Someone with particularly fond memories of a favorite grandmother's garden usually will respond to similar gardens throughout his or her lives with love and longing. As the eye is trained artistically, it learns when a landscape or garden has achieved the subtle balance and harmony that make it beautiful in a formal sense. There are a set of design principles taught in art schools that reveal the nature of these balances and harmonies: Compositions look stable when they are built on pyramids. Symmetry is boring; asymmetry has movement. Two lines have harmonious proportions when the shorter line is to the longer one as the longer one is to both lines laid end to end. Several smaller masses balance one larger one.

But going to art school is not necessary to acquire a feeling for harmony. Most adults acquire this sense of fittingness or balance simply by living in a world—both natural and human-built—that embodies these rules in its design, rules primarily based on information from the sense of sight. One need not be Japanese to see the beauty in a well-designed Japanese garden, where such balances and harmonies have been exquisitely worked out.

Our notions of beauty are thus both innate and acquired. We experience them all through the sense of sight. The more we learn about how and why we see beauty, the better gardeners we will become, and the more sophisticated our appreciation of gardens will be.

An amateur is often critical or at least uninterested in that which he does not understand. Appreciation comes with knowledge. To enhance our appreciation of gardens, we need to examine their formal artistic qualities one by one to learn what they have to teach us.

C OLOR AND ITS PERCEPTIONS

ABOVE. *There is red—and then there is red. Toward the blue end of the spectrum we get magenta. Its electric effect makes it a bright color in the garden, and famously hard to coordinate with other colors if quiet, serene effects are wanted. This bougainvillea, growing in a well-patinaed pot in the Wesley Rouse Garden at Pine Meadow Gardens in Southbury, Connecticut, defines the color.*

OPPOSITE. *Guess the mood inspired by these colors before you finish reading this caption. The photograph of 'Angelique' tulips and* Viola *'Crystal Blub' was taken at the Atlantic Botanic Garden in Atlanta, Georgia. If you guessed the sweet sorrow of love lost, we are on the same wavelength.*

We merely think that we see trees and walkways and grass. All we really see is color, shape, and size. Everything else is our interpretation of what we see. The French Impressionist painters used their knowledge of this fact to produce marvels of color. They worked to reproduce color without preconceptions, and they painted the truth. Their colors still melt on the canvas under the century-old sun, still make us breathless with their air and light and humidity, or soothe us with their flowers and foliage.

To create better gardens and better appreciate the ones we have, we need to pay close attention to colors and how they are used—when they are pleasing and when they grate, what they mean to us and how they affect our moods.

Colors might be said to have different ranges. There is, of course, the familiar gradation from violet to red—the spectrum of the rainbow. But there are also ranges of intensity, from the chromatic colors to pale pastels, darker shades mixed with black; a spectrum of moods, running from somber dark purples to cheery bright yellows; and a range of heat, from the coldest ice-blue to red hot.

For gardening purposes, one of the most important of these scales is visibility, or brightness. Every color has a property called tone, which is its inherent brightness under standard illumination. Yellow is the most visible color, followed by yellow-orange. Greenish yellow and orange are about equal in tone, followed in order by orange-red, red, green, blue-green, red-violet, blue, blue-violet, and violet. It is a well-known gardening rule that areas of equal visibility or light intensity should be separated by contrasting areas of either lighter or darker

foliage. One might separate drifts of bright yellow *Helianthus* and coreopsis with a dark green mugho pine, for instance, or drifts of dark-foliaged plants with a clump of artemisias.

Gardens are not seen under standard illumination, however; they are seen in all kinds of light, from the pale, pink morning light to the purplish light before a thunderstorm. The kind and amount of light on a garden has a lot to do with our perception of it and which colors in it command our attention.

As the sun heads down on a clear summer afternoon, it often throws a warm light on the garden. Surfaces do not glint as much; highlights are not as diamond hard. Yellows soften and warm to apricot colors, while the greens of the foliage become darker and richer. Reds darken considerably as the light begins to fail. The sun eventually sets, and the world enters the gloaming. Then the blues, lavenders, and violets begin to glow, sometimes almost impossibly so. I first became aware of this phenomenon when walking one twilit evening in my perennial garden. A drift of *Platycodon grandiflorus* 'Blue' by the side of the path was in full flower. The wide-open bells glowed with a cold, deep intensity in the dim light. Subsequently, it became apparent that all the other lavender to violet flowers were glowing, too.

This change in perception has to do with the way our eyes are made. When light enters the eye, it forms an image on the retina at the back of the eyeball. The retina has two types of optically sensitive cells. The rods see light intensity but do not distinguish colors, while the cones respond to the different wavelengths of color. The cones are most sensitive in daylight; their efficacy diminishes as night falls. As darkness intensifies, we see fewer colors and more intensity. The cones are not able to distinguish wavelengths, but the rods continue to see mass and some light and shadow.

The wavelengths in the visible-light spectrum run from 4,000 angstroms (blue) to slightly less than 10,000 angstroms (red). The retina's maximum sensitivity during daylight occurs at 5,550 units. As night falls, its maximum sensitivity shifts toward the blue (shorter wavelengths) and occurs at about 5,000 angstroms. Under low light, reds turn dark and blues seem much brighter.

We can use this optical information creatively in the garden. Blue and lavender flowers should be placed where they get dappled shade during the day, and in a place where one walks in the evening twilight. Conversely, sunny spots are good places for rich chromatic colors, especially the deep reds of favorite scented roses.

ABOVE. *At dusk when blue-violet becomes relatively much brighter, it is a good idea to have it represented close to the house. In this private garden at Chipping Camden, England, the gardener has planted violet campanulas among the red coral bells to light one's steps in the gloaming.*

OPPOSITE. *Violet can also be quite subdued, as shown by the explosion of puffy ceanothus at the garden of Madame d'Andlau in Remalard, France. Notice the excellent color coordination with the shutters. It would be inappropriate if the color of the shutters was brighter than the ceanothus.*

ABOVE. *Our perception of colors is affected by nearby colors. The medium-dark green of these rose leaves appears brighter when seen with the bright yellow 'Fruhlingsgold' roses than it would with deep red roses.*

ABOVE. *A rich knowledge of plants, flowers, and color harmonies produced this exquisite border at Hadspen Garden in Somerset, England. The color key is struck by the deliciously orange Oriental Poppy (*Papaver orientale *'Henfield Brilliant'). Yellow-orange roses sing high harmony and the low-growing Rock Rose (*Helianthemum nummularium*) hits the ruddy bass notes.*

ABOVE. *These Japanese maple (*Acer palmatum*) leaves burst into a fiery glow when backlit by the sun. They would look far different if lit from the top, and would turn a dark, murky red in the failing light of dusk.*

ABOVE. *The subtle, warm color of terra cotta makes an excellent partner for cool flower colors like these lavender ground morning glories* (Convolvulus mauritanicus).

PAGES 32-33. *Green appears darker when seen with the violet and dark blue flowers of geraniums, lupines, bearded iris, and catmint* (Nepeta mussinii), *as these views display, at the garden of Levans Hall, Kendal, England.*

ENTRANCING COLOR EFFECTS

The colors in an artist's paint palette are quite different functionally from those of colored light. The primary colors of pigment are red, yellow, and blue, but the primaries of light are red, violet, and green. Mix all the paint pigments together, and you get a muddy blackish brown. Project the pure primaries as beams of light on the same spot on a screen together, and you get white light. Besides these primaries, there are also the colors of vision: the colors as we perceive them and as they act and react together in our eye. And these colors of vision are most important when creating color harmonies in the garden.

There are four primaries of vision: red, yellow, blue, and green. Here are the colors they produce when mixed:

- Red and yellow: orange.
- Yellow and green: leaf green.
- Green and blue: turquoise.
- Blue and red: violet.
- Red, blue, and yellow: reddish-brown.
- Red, yellow, and green: yellow-brown.
- Yellow, green, and blue: green ish brown.
- Green, blue, and red: bluish brown.
- All the colors: black.

Notice that when three colors are mixed, we start to get the earth tones, the leaf colors, the colors of rock and bark and soil.

Besides the physical changes in our sight that create special effects in the garden, there are also optical changes of color. Complementary colors appear more vivid when together than when viewed apart, thanks to a process called successive contrast. Our eye actually sees them as intensified and enriched, exaggerating their differences. Yellow is more yellow and violet more violet when the two colors share a common boundary.

Simultaneous contrast is a related phenomenon in which two colors abutting each other are subtly changed by their proximity as they acquire a hazy wash of their complementaries. An intense, pure color will begin to glow with a halo of its complement when stared at for a time. This phenomenon is also responsible for the complementary colors that appear as afterimages. That is, when a person stares at a chromatically colored image and then looks quickly away at a neutral-colored wall or piece of paper, an afterimage appears colored with the complementaries of the original. This phenomenon explains why artist Jasper Johns painted an American flag in orange, white, and green; its afterimage is red, white, and blue!

A color's hue may be subtly changed by the other colors it is seen with; for example, green seen with yellow looks warmer and is more visible than green seen with blue. Also remember that most flower colors are not pure. Apple blossoms are white flushed with pink. Pale yellow flowers appear to be the color of butter in their shady portions. Gaillardia petals have a

mixture of several colors. Try to paint an ordinary daylily (*Hemerocallis fulva*) and you will soon see that you need a palette full of colors to suggest the golden throats and subtle salmons and oranges of the petals.

Color harmonies among just a few plants will be lost when the plants can only be viewed at a distance. So place small groups with interesting color harmonies close to a path, patio, or walkway. Large areas of color can be distinguished at a distance, but from far away they will tend toward a more muted blue or gray tone.

Studies have shown that optical discords and harmonies tend to affect people the same way all around the world. Most people react positively when colors harmonize, and most also get a disturbing feeling of discord when colors clash.

As a general rule, colors close to one another on the color wheel harmonize. The farther away on the wheel they are, the greater their potential to clash, until the complementary color is reached across the wheel. Equal areas of complementary colors tend to fight with one another, but these colors can be harmonized by one of two means. You may attenuate (dilute) one of the colors with white to make a soft pastel, or use one of the colors very sparingly, as an accent. For instance, a bed of optically energetic orange California poppies butting up against a bed of optically active blue lobelia would rattle one's retina for sure. But picture that rich blue touching a row of light-cream–colored roses. The orange is tamed by mixing it with white, and as a creamy pastel, it combines perfectly with the deep blue. Or picture just one California poppy blooming in that sea of blue lobelia, accenting it, relieving its wide expanse of blue.

The general rule above is not hard and fast. Sometimes mixing in a white flower to create a pastel will set up a clash. Orange and red, for instance, are next to each other on the wheel, and they make a harmonic—if hot!—combination. But mix the red with white to make a light, clear

OPPOSITE TOP. *This otherworldly landscape at the desert garden at Huntington Gardens in San Marino, California, contains several types of aloes—big, bruising cousins of the common* Aloe vera *we grow on our kitchen windowsills. Different shapes share the peculiarly rich oranges and flame reds that characterize this genus's flowers.*

OPPOSITE BOTTOM. *Plants that share variations on a color can be very effective together, especially when their shapes are also interesting and varied. In this private Connecticut garden, earth colors are the main color theme, stated by the dried, brown flower clusters of* Hydrangea quercifolia *at the bottom. The just-emerging, flowering plumes of tall miscanthus grass restate the theme in a slightly different way at the top. At right, the beige-to-white flowering spikes of* Cimicifuga racemosa *state the theme as a very pale pastel.*

RIGHT. *Color moves us emotionally, which is why a white garden is so powerfully ironic—exuberant in form yet silent in color. A white garden of exceptional beauty is the Mrs. Hendricks Garden in Atlanta, Georgia, shown in the photograph. A* Deutzia gracilis *opens little galaxies of stars along its arching branches at bottom, set off by a stand of 'Maureen' tulips. The arching stems, this time of* Viburnum macrocephalum, *are decorated with white flower balls at top.*

ABOVE. *Sumptuous hedonism and reckless energy is the mood of this combination of wax begonia, petunia, pelargonium, verbena, and fuchsia beneath a windowbox with tuberous begonias at Butchart Gardens in Victoria, Canada.*

pink, and orange will seem a heavy-handed color combined with it. Pink is somehow more delicate, calling for a clear light blue or a soothing lavender. The two permanent clashes are pink with orange and light yellow-green with purple. These mixtures can always be counted on to clash, and if you use them, do so because you want a clash.

I discovered an important rule one day at the Philadelphia Flower Show. I was looking at rows of flower arrangements set out for judging when it struck me that all the arrangements shared a certain design principle for combining flowers by color. The flower colors were related by certain shared hues. That is, some color in a flower was either shared or closely related to a color in its neighbor. Such an arrangement ties the flowers together and shows taste and careful consideration. The pretty pink flowers of potentilla 'Miss Willmott', for example, can be associated with the white-flowered, tuberous begonia 'Red Picotee'. The center of the potentilla flower is a dark, rich red that perfectly matches the picotee edge of the white begonia blooms.

How do we coordinate all those muddy colors in the middle, made from mixtures of all the hues: the dark umbers, browns, ochres, brownish greens, muds, beiges, yellow-greens, and burnt colors? These are the colors of foliage, of the earth, of rocks, of mulch, of dead plants, and old leaves. They are the great separators of clear colors, and chief among them is green.

When we view the world, or our gardens, most of what we see is green. Other colors are usually located here and there. Green separates other colors, keeps clashes apart, sets off beds of color, and keeps things restful and cool. For every chromatic color in the garden, there must be a hundred different shades of green. Not only that, but flowering herbaceous perennials tend to go in and out of color over just a few weeks, although other types of plants, such as annuals, can flower profusely all season. So even the flowering plants are mostly green most of the time.

For this reason, combining plants for their foliage color is a good strategy. If we put together good foliage harmonies first, and coordinate colors second, we will have good-looking gardens over the whole season. Just concentrating on flower color, without taking the foliage into consideration, tends to give unlooked-for—and often unpleasant—results.

Foliage color harmonies occur naturally because most foliage is some shade of green. What varies most from plant to plant is the value or intensity of the green. Look at any mixed border of garden shrubs, or visit a natural place where many different woody plants are growing. Squint at the scene until the masses of foliage become lumpy shapes with no definition. You will be able to see the light intensities of the various foliages much more easily. Note which plants have bright green foliage, and which seem to absorb light and turn dark. The horse chestnut tree (*Aesculus hippocastanum*) has dark, light-absorbing leaves, for instance, while the yellowwood (*Cladrastis lutea*) has bright yellow-green leaves. Purple-leaved plants are the darkest, while gray-green or silvery green leaves are usually among the brightest.

Mixing in lots of silver, blue-green, or white foliage helps relieve these greens and breaks up the picture without disturbing the color harmony. When considering shrubs and permanent plants, such as perennials for a border, make a list of the plants according to foliage brightness, and then mix them. Use the medium-valued plants as a background, and plant them here and there with dark-leaved and light-leaved plants. Such changes from bright to dark green help set the garden's mood. Be sure to stagger your planting in a natural-looking way; regularly spaced plants of contrasting value can give a clumsy effect.

Colors suggest moods. A black-and-white line drawing may convey quite different moods when copies of it are colored differently. As the Impressionists showed us that color is the visual component of physical reality, the Expressionists demonstrated how color can also be the stuff of our inner, psychological reality. This is not color as we see it in the outer world. Look at Ernst Kirchner's putrid, chartreuse faces, his angry, ripping use of red. It is not the physical world that is depicted here, but a tormented state of mind. We have known it all along: envy is green, anger is red, depression is blue, cheerfulness is yellow, purity is white, mystery and mourning are black. A single color conveys a single mood, but a more complex mood is suggested by a group of colors.

A flowering garden can be

planned to convey a mood. The fun is in choosing the plants and designing the garden; the danger is that it will look amateurish if you become too literal. A large garden can hold wide swaths of dramatic color. An intimate garden needs more carefully chosen plants and colors if it is not to be garish. Be subtle in a small space, bold in a large one. Lovely pale pink bells of *Bergenia cordifolia* emerging from clouds of blue *Myosotis* in spring, or pink roses with the clear light blue of Cape plumbago, suggest a heavenly mood of hopefulness. The dark blue-violet flowers and dark green leaves of monkshood (*Aconitum napellus*) combined with ferns and the airy lavender puffs of *Thalictrum aquilegifolium* convey a somber but poetic mood.

ABOVE. *Magenta can be toned down and softened into the lovely red-pink-lavender given by this heath (*Erica carnea *'Pirbright Rose'), in which case its visual impact is muted. The rhododendron is 'Rose Blewett'. The scene is at the Van Dusen Botanical Garden, in Vancouver, Canada.*

ABOVE. *The hard, bright magenta pink of* Cosmos bipinnatus *makes up in exuberance what it lacks in subtlety. Even so, such colors are best relegated to the back of a garden.*

OPPOSITE. *An oft-chosen color scheme is no color scheme, but rather the helter-skelter look of the cottage garden, where plants are installed because they are colorful, and not much thought is given to where or why. Even master colorists love the spontaneous, fun, and cheerful effects that result, as this example at Monet's Garden in Giverny, France, demonstrates.*

I like to choose a mood as a garden theme by thinking of a favorite film. *Casablanca,* for instance, is a movie with a hot, desperate mood. The hero, Rick, seems restrained, but we can see that on the inside he is full of paranoia, pain, and suffering. Despite the suffering, Rick is still capable of a noble act that redeems the wartime hell the characters inhabit. To catch this subtle mood in a garden, one could be literal and construct a garden of white walls, sand, and desert plants. Voilà! A little bit of the old Casbah right in your own backyard.

Another approach is to let your imagination go. Be poetic rather than literal. Think hot, desperate: the trumpet vine's ability to tear apart walls, throwing off hot-looking blooms in the heat of summer. Or perhaps bittersweet (*Celastrus scandens*) is even better. Its yellow-orange capsules split open to reveal shiny red berries in the fall, when the beauty of summer has faded.

Such moods can be enhanced by some carefully considered paint. Picture the bittersweet climbing up a white garage wall; it inches toward a window with a sash painted the same green as its light green leaves, accented by a thin line of berry-red piping painted on the lower sill. You may even like to paint the wooden underside of the roof projection the same green.

Few of us feel we have the time to make such careful adjustments, but following up on these design inspirations is worth the effort. Although painting the window sash the color of bittersweet foliage may pay off for just a few weeks in the fall, for those

few weeks your wall will be a work of art. Seed your property with several of these artistic happenings and keep quiet about it. You will soon find out who is attuned to your horticultural and sculptural visions and who is not.

Because the range of garden colors is just about infinite, so are the chances for superior color harmonies. Keep your eyes open for appealing combinations, and take notes wherever they occur—in gardens, in paintings, in magazines.

Once, while digging in my vegetable garden, I found a broken piece of an old cup with tantalizing fragments of color: earthy green, pure deep blue, and muted scarlet under a clear, fired glaze. I imagined the whole as having once had a simple but elegant floral design. I kept the piece of crockery and used its appealing color scheme to make a passage in the perennial bed that included one large bugloss (*Anchusa azurea* 'Royal Blue') with intense blue flowers on three-foot branching spikes, surrounded by several clumps of two-foot-tall, muted scarlet carnations (*Dianthus caryophyllus* 'English Giants'), all interspersed with the earthy green leaves of lady's-mantle (*Alchemilla mollis*) underneath. The blue accented the scarlet, and it was all held to earth by the lady's-mantle. The colors were strong but sparingly used because the garden was small.

COLOR HARMONY: STRATEGIES AND SUGGESTIONS

The successful use of color in a garden involves not just the contribution of the artist's eye for color, but also the more practical skills of a plantsperson, agronomist, pest-control specialist, farmer, gardener, landscape designer, garden designer, and irrigation specialist.

One final skill is that of the pathfinder for your own ideas. When it comes to combining colors, you are the boss, and whatever appeals to you is best for your garden. Color likes and dislikes are individual; do not be afraid to use your favorite colors. It does not make any difference what others say. Artists who consistently please themselves in the face of constant criticism and misunderstanding are often innovators. Your ideas might stand the horticultural world on its ear, but you will never know unless you follow through, implement your own innovations, and maintain them long enough to be noticed.

Designs that are too crazy, however, are usually less than pleasing. If you aim to please others as well as yourself, you will do well to keep in mind a few rules of thumb.

• A small area of strong color accents a wide area of harmonizing pastels. One clump of strong red bee balm (*Monarda didyma*), for example, accents a wide patch of pale yellow *Achillea taygetea* 'Moonshine'. The pale lavender of wisteria is accented by 'Red Emperor' tulips.

• Harmonizing pastels tend to drift into one another. Drifts are areas of the same plant that taper at either end so they merge smoothly into one another through the garden bed. Some favorite pastel color combinations for the perennial border:
  Pink *Dicentra spectabilis* with blue *Polemonium reptans*
  Blue *Myosotis sylvatica* and yellow *Alyssum saxatile*
  Yellow daylilies (*Hemerocallis* spp.) and lavender lupines (*Lupinus polyphyllus*)
  Lavender Russian sage (*Perovskia triplicifolia*) and pink bee balm (*Monarda didyma* 'Croftway Pink')
• Reds and oranges "leap out" visually; green is neutral and restful; blues and violets tend to recede from the other colors. You can suggest a deeper garden by placing the reds in

ABOVE. *Reds and oranges leap out visually to the observer, as demonstrated by these 'Gudoshnik' tulips growing around a birch tree at Roozengaarde Display Gardens in Mount Vernon, Washington.*

OPPOSITE. *Something sensuous—and yet at the same time sacred—is suggested by the provocative color and design of this garden. A weeping-willow-leaved pear (*Pyrus salicifolia* 'Pendula') flares with a spiritual energy that dissipates through the zigzagging borders of* Saxifraga umbrosa *'Elliott's Variety' at the garden of Frank and Marjorie Lawley at Herterton House, England.*

the foreground and the blues in the background; conversely, you can foreshorten the garden by planting the blues up front and the reds behind.

• Take note of the color variations within individual flowers and repeat them by choosing other flowers with similar colors. Choose one of the minor internal colors of the daylily (*Hemerocallis fulva*), for example, and select a companion whose major color echoes it, such as a golden *Heliopsis scabra* 'Karat'.

• When making color associations, emphasize the visually strong colors in large areas of their pastel tints: use a light lemon or pastel moonshine for yellow; pink or very light carmine for red; cream or buff for orange. Accent these with small areas of pure, intense blue, such as *Clematis heracleifolia* or the annual bachelor's buttons. Conversely, use shades or tones of the visually recessive colors: purple or maroon or dusky violet for blue, with accents of bright yellow or scarlet.

TOP AND LEFT. *Silvery-leaved* Artemisia ludoviciana *grows with a pink scabiosa in the Penny Vogel Garden in Estacada, Oregon (left). The same color scheme is arrayed very differently, with a different emotional impact, in the photo above, where artemisia grows with* Lavatera trimestris *at the Gianangelo Herb Garden on San Juan Island in Washington.*

OPPOSITE. *Blue-green is a quiet, recessive color, as shown by its muted presence on Adirondack chairs and woodwork at the Lisa Stamm Garden on Shelter Island, New York. The mirror reflects a sunnier portion of the place.*

COLORS AND THE OTHER SENSES

While the names we give to primary colors are specific and unique, the various shades and tints of the mixtures tend to be named after things that recall other elements of nature or the other senses: orange, olive, apricot, and plum; coral, salmon, and peacock green; rose, lavender, and lilac; turquoise, sapphire, and ruby; ochre, slate-gray, and sand.

Pleasant aromas, such as rose, lilac, violet, coffee, orange, and vanilla, are closely associated with colors, as are some flavors, such as orange, lemon, chocolate, burgundy, and cherry. The French poet Baudelaire wrote that "perfumes, colors, and sounds are interchangeable. There are perfumes fresh as the flesh of babies, sweet as oboes, and green as the prairies."

The harmonies associated with smells and tastes can give us a clue to color harmonies that are useful in the garden. Chocolate and vanilla are excellent flavors together, and so the dark, chocolate-colored (and chocolate-scented!) flowers of *Cosmos atrosanguineus* harmonize perfectly with the vanilla-white leaves of *Senecio cineraria*. Orange and lemon go together not just in sorbets but also in the garden—when a large area of *Coreopsis verticillata* 'Moonbeam' grows with the vivid red-orange accents of *Crocosmia pottsii*.

Different types of sounds, too, are associated with colors: blue notes, red-hot horns, and "Mood Indigo." The very words used to describe

ABOVE. Weigela 'Looymansii Aurea' has foliage the same color as a flavor: lime. The photo was taken at the garden of Mr. and Mrs. M. Perry at Bosvigo House, Truro, England.

OPPOSITE. Colors change with the time of day. Here late in the afternoon in a private garden designed by Isabel Green in Santa Barbara, California, the sun sinks toward the ocean and the trees radiate an emerald glow in the backlighting. Reds turn dark. Yellow is muted. But the blue-violet convolvulus in the foreground will begin to glow in the halflight.

PAGES 46-47. There comes a time of day when the light of evening takes a final bow and mutes the colors of the garden, as here at the Donald M. Kendall Sculpture Garden, in Purchase, New York.

color come from sound and music: chromatic, tone, harmony, dissonance, pure, muddy. Certain words describing sound have their correspondence in color, too. Timbre, or the distinctive quality of a sound given by its overtones, relates to the texture of a colored surface; pitch relates to hue. Many musicians and color theorists over the years have devised systems whereby notes on the musical scale are assigned colors. The simplest music-color system is probably that devised by Sir Isaac Newton, using the familiar notes of the diatonic scale.

Color	Major Scale	Note
Red	C	Do
Orange	D	Re
Yellow	E	Mi
Green	F	Fa
Blue	G	So
Indigo	A	La
Violet	B	Ti

Using Newton's system, you can base a color scheme in the garden on a simple melodic phrase. For instance, "Mary Had a Little Lamb" is given by A–G–F–G–A–A–A: indigo and blue, colored with green. Monkshood and nepeta in a sea of green leaves. It works.

Aleksandr Scriabin, the nineteenth--century Russian composer, came up with the following system:

Note	Color
C	Red
G	Rosy orange
D	Yellow
A	Green
E	Baby blue
B	Moonshine
F-sharp	Bright blue
D-flat	Violet
A-flat	Purple
E-flat	Metallic
B-flat	Metallic
F	Dark red

Musical scales made of half steps are called chromatic. In music, "chromatic" also means those half-step notes foreign to a key that are used to color that key. It is thus easy to see why composers might assign actual colors to notes. We can check this system easily by choosing a chord and looking at the colors of its notes. One such might be C–F–G, which would be red, dark red, and rosy orange in Scriabin's system. The complementary color and chromatic note to this series would be A, or green. One could certainly choose flower and foliage colors to reproduce that effect in the garden. And one more: D–G–A translates to rosy orange, yellow, and green. The complement to these would be blue, which Scriabin assigns to E.

Color enters our consciousness through the eye, and sound through the ear, but they are both vibratory phenomena, dependent on our senses for their perception. Color is the wavelength of light, and sound the wavelength of vibrations in air. As such, color and sound are not so much physical "things" as qualities of things. The color of a flower is not something physical that can be separated from that flower, but arises in our eye as a consequence of the way light is differentially absorbed and reflected by the flower. Similarly, sound is not perceived until vibrations reach the cochleas in our ears.

Because color happens "in here" instead of "out there," it changes as our perceptions change. The color we see in full daylight can be quite different in the early morning, in the evening, after sunset, at night, and in the rain. It also differs by its proximity to other colors, and its perception can depend on our mood.

White, because of its neutrality, is very susceptible to mood change in the garden. In sunlight, it intensifies the colors around it. In partial shade, it stands out while other colors recede. In full shade, it brightens the shadows and dark greens around it and stands out even more. In the deep shade of the woodlands in the Middle Atlantic states, bugbane (*Cimicifuga racemosa*) is frequently found growing wild. Its tall, slender white spires glow in the darkness like candles, adding some interest to what otherwise would be undifferentiated pools of shadow. Its effect is most dramatic when strong full sunlight deepens the shade, less so when overcast weather scatters the light and softens the contrasts between the shady and lighted portions of the woods.

White is present not only in flowers, but also in white, gray, or silver leaves. Some plants, like certain cultivars of hosta, have green leaves with white variegations, and these white streakings are subject to the same phenomena that affect all-white foliage.

ABOVE. *Yellow-flowered* Viola glabella, *violet-flowered* Vinca minor, *and boxwood* (Buxus sempervirens) *form an almost contiguous mass of barely differentiated foliage swirling around the base of a tree in Deepwood Gardens, Salem, Oregon.*

WORKING WITH FOLIAGE

Since most of the garden is green most of the time, it helps the overall appearance if the various greens of the foliage are used to augment flower color. Too often gardeners focus solely on flower color, allowing the greens to occur haphazardly, but green is the color that pulls everything together and deserves to be planned.

Leaf color ranges from deep, dark, almost blackish green to very light yellow-green. Most leaves, however, are a medium green: straightforward, cheerful, down-to-earth. Then there are the leaves that stray altogether from green. We find foliage ranging from white and silver through gray, blue-green, to blue; from bronze through red; from light yellow to golden, and through the permutations and combinations of the variegated leaves.

When most people think of a garden, they think of its flowers, walks and paths, trees and woody trunks, and only secondarily its leaves. But almost everything we see in a garden is leaves. Good leaf combinations alone can make a beautiful garden. The variegated *Hakonechloa macra variegata* 'Aureola' is a Japanese-looking grasslike plant of exceptional beauty that looks best in light shade, where it will associate well with the wide, smooth leaves of hostas and the neat tufts of fernlike creeping Jacob's ladder (*Polemonium reptans*). Such a combination, chosen for the leaves and their textures, will look even better out of bloom than when the *Polemonium* hangs out its soft, blue bells in spring. Leaf colors work better in association with certain flower colors and less well with others.

The aesthetic appreciation of color that we achieve through the sense of sight ordinarily depends on the relationship of colors, rather than on the appreciation of a single color by itself. In the bird world, it is the vermilion shafts that breathe life into the blackish brown feathers of the northern flicker. The blush of blue *Phlox divaricata* freshens the whites of spring, and the pale gold lily touches the heart even more when it is set among the billowing, muted gray-green leaves of 'Silver King' artemisia (*Artemisia ludoviciana albula*), with intense blue accents provided by blue flax (*Linum perenne*). The question is not just what our favorite colors are, but what our favorite color combinations are.

In my garden planning, I start with the color combinations I like best: a champagne gold and jade green, found in the flowers of the thornless Lady Banks rose (*Rosa banksia)* and the leaves of *Pittosporum crassifolium*—two plants that grow well together. Then I add colors to a pairing: the green needs the contrast of a dark plant, perhaps a conifer like mugho pine or an evergreen perennial like *Helleborus orientalis.*

Here is a very general guide that can help you plan for foliage–flower combinations in the garden.

• Medium green: Most plants have medium green foliage, and almost any flower color works well with it. Bright yellow and medium green are often found together, and the only caveat for the gardener is to avoid too much of this rather common association.

• Dark green: Among the herbaceous perennials, two types of monkshood, *Aconitum napellus* and *Aconitum carmichaelii*, have true dark green leaves. Familiar plants with dark green leaves include yew, *Acanthus*, holly, cotoneaster, some hostas, rhododendron, and many of the needle-leaf evergreens. These dark-leaved plants form backdrops for brighter plants in the foreground, and for lighter flower colors, including white, with which they associate well. Deep shades of blue, purple, blue-green, or violet tend to recede and be lost among dark-leaved plants. Rich reds, oranges, and yellows will stand out against the dark leaves. Dark foliage will emphasize lighter tints and pastels of all the colors, including blue.

• Bright green: Catalpa, lawn grasses, *Myosotis sylvatica*, *Sedum spectabile*, many tulips, and innumerable other plants have bright green leaves. These plants associate well with orange, pale yellow, darker red and burgundy, light lavender, and bright blue. Violet, purple, and dark lavender tend to get lost when used with bright green foliage, as do white flowers.

• Silver to gray: Some junipers, the *Artemisias*, *Elaeagnus* 'Coral Silver', *Santolina*, *Achillea*, *Cerastium tomentosum*, *Lavandula*, *Lychnis coronaria*, *Nepeta faassenii*, *Ruta graveolens*, *Salvia argentea*, *Verbascum*, some *Sedums*, *Sempervivums*, *Senecio cineraria*, *Stachys byzantina*,

and *Veronica incana* are all well-known plants with leaves in the silver-white-gray region. These plants are all extremely useful in the landscape to separate areas of color, to relieve wide areas of green, to contrast with dark-foliaged plants, and to associate with clear, bright, chromatic flower colors of all kinds. They are less successfully paired with very light pastels and tints, and white flowers, which get lost against the light leaves. Very dark colors, however, especially dark reds and red-browns, look exceptionally beautiful paired with contrasting silver-leaved plants.

• Blue to blue-green: Blue spruce (*Picea pungens* cultivars), the huge western juniper (*Juniperus occidentalis*), the blue forms of *Chamaecyparis lawsoniana*, some kinds of

ABOVE. *Few plants have more interesting leaf variegations than hostas, and few hostas are as interesting as the 'Gold Standard' variety, here growing with pure white impatiens at Pine Meadow Gardens in Southbury, Connecticut.*

PAGES 50-51. *Lush green and gold foliage mounds are the strong feature in Frank and Marjorie Lawley's garden at Herterton House, England. Interestingly—and very uniquely—the Lawleys have planted areas of pure color in the troughs between the mounds. Iris, violas, and oriental poppies supply the blues and red that are given context and visual oomph by the preponderance of foliage. Notice the absence of yellow flowers, unneeded since the color is already supplied by some of the leaves.*

ABOVE. *Sometimes it is not the color itself, but the relationship of colors in a garden that makes a scene exquisitely beautiful. White calla lily accents the pinks, magentas, and red-violets in the photo.* Clematis *'Dr. Ruppal', at the left, is planted near dark violet* Geranium sanguineum *and light* Geranium lancastriense *at the Geoff Beasley Garden in Sherwood, Oregon.*

eucalyptuses, blue fescue (*Festuca glauca*), and blue oat grass (*Helictotrichon sempervirens*) are familiar plants with distinctly bluish foliage. They tend to recede in the landscape because of their shy color, but they associate nicely with white- to gray-leaved plants, and especially with clear, shell-pink roses or intense reds.

• Bronze, red, or purplish: Plants with leaves ranging from orange-bronze to purple include red-leaved *Acer palmatum, Corylus maxima* 'Purpurea', *Cotinus coggygria* 'Purpureus', red-leaved *Fagus sylvatica,* red-leaved *Prunus cerasifera, Corylus avellana* 'Fusco-Rubra', *Ajuga reptans, Astilbe* 'Fanal', canna lilies, *Lobelia fulgens, Rheum palmatum, Rodgersia pinnata* 'Superba', purple *Salvia officinalis, Pennisetum setaceum* 'Cupreum', red- to orange-leaved *Phormium tenax, Sedum maximum* 'Atropurpureum', and *Sedum spurium* 'Dragon's Blood'. These plants associate well with the contrasting colors of yellow, turquoise, blue, white, and the light pinks, but are less effective as the flower colors come closer to the foliage hue.

• Golden: Plants with bright yellow to golden foliage include many deciduous and evergreen types, including this sampling of garden favorites: *Acer japonicum* 'Aureum', *Chamaecyparis lawsoniana, Robinia pseudoacacia* 'Frisia', *Thuja plicata* 'Aurea', *Chrysanthemum parthenium* 'Aureum', *Hakonechloa macra* 'Aureola', several of the hostas, many junipers, golden *Ligustrum,* golden *Salvia officinalis,* several of the *Taxus baccata* varieties, *Thuja occidentalis* 'Rheingold', and many others. Golden leaves contrast nicely with blues, from deep purples to light baby blue and mauve. They also work well with red, dark red, brown, and, surprisingly, with yellow flowers for an all-yellow theme. Orange and cream are less successful, and white flowers tend to wash out when surrounded by gold.

• Variegated: *Acer negundo* 'Variegatum', several of the *Cornus* species, *Fagus sylvatica* 'Tricolor', some hollies, plus dozens and dozens of familiar shrubs and perennials have variegated forms (often called "*variegatum*") with white or yellow markings. The best way to use these forms is to place them with plants that have solid green to dark green leaves, giving them an architectural appearance that helps define the garden's structure. If you are going to use colored flowers along with the variegated forms, work with the colors in the foliage: white flowers with white variegations, yellow with yellow, and so forth. Keep the strong colors, such as golden-leaved plants or those with bright white variegations (such as the *Acer negundo*), toward the center of your landscape; use the darker-leaved plants to shade off into adjoining areas. (Edging your landscape with bright plants emphasizes its edges and makes it separate from the surrounding territory.) If you do not define the edges, your garden will look larger and will "borrow" territory from surrounding landscaping.

Good planning for a colorful garden means keeping a notebook in your pocket or purse and jotting down the plants you like and the color combinations that impress you. Find those plants at the nurseries so you become familiar with them as seedlings as well as in their maturity. See how other people use them. Look for choice specimens or cultivars. Try them in your garden, and if they work as you remembered, keep them. Otherwise, separate them or give them away.

Creating color combinations that work takes a great deal of time. Unlike an artist at his easel, a gardener who rearranges or changes color must then wait for nature to catch up to his design—and transplanting plants usually has at least a one-year lag time before the plant sends out strong roots and makes a large enough plant to put on a mature flower show. The painter can quickly scrape away an offending area with a palette knife, but the garden arranger must remove a plant and put in another—and these new plants seldom come covered with blossoms.

If you are rearranging for color, try to keep your transplanting for the early spring, when the soil thaws out but precious little is up and about. In the summer and fall, keep a log of which plants need to be moved, and then when the spring arrives, go to work. In the early spring, the air temperature is cool and pleasant to work in, the soil more easily worked, and the plants mostly still dormant and often in need of a move and a crown division in the bargain. If there is too much work, reflect on why heaven makes teenage boys. If you stand there and direct the boys, they can do a passable

job for a modest amount of money.

Most plants do not feel dramatic effects of being moved in early spring, so bloom ordinarily will not be interrupted. Be aware, though, that plants with long tap roots resent transplanting at any time, and those that bloom very early in the spring should be moved in late fall, before the soil freezes.

ABOVE. *Coreopsis verticillata 'Moonbeam' and sun-gold heleniums relate to the moon-dust color of blue lime grass. As appealing as these plants are together, they are brought to life by the dark red drumstick alliums (*Allium sphaerocephalum*) in a private garden in Southampton, New York, designed by Tish Rehill and Michael Daughterty.*

PAGES 54-55. *The eye is filled with a marvelous mixture of strong topiary shapes, subtle color combinations, hard lines, and soft natural forms at Levans Hall, Kendall, in England.*

 ORM

Some forms mean little or nothing to us: the amorphous shape of a mass of flotsam in a tidal eddy, for instance. Others are packed with essential information and are quite potent when we see them: the forms of foods when we are hungry, the forms of cars growing larger as they approach us on the highway, the shape of a beautiful body.

Form gives definition to the objects on which the colors of the world are painted; if color is the spirit of a thing, form is the body. We discern form through visual cues given to us by mass and line. Color and texture then aid us in further identification of forms. As we will subsequently see, these concepts become important in planning the garden. Mass is visualized through contrasts in value between light and dark areas, whether colored or not. Where two objects have about the same light value as one another, the distinguishing lines are blurred and indistinct, masses run together, it is difficult to tell figure from ground, and forms become hard to interpret. Where they make a striking contrast, as when a black hat is seen resting on a white table, line is sharp, mass is distinct, the figure jumps out from the ground, and we can more easily recognize what we see.

Background and form are capable of trading places in optical illusions—and so altering the meaning of what we see. In a familiar example, a vase is the figure, seen against a contrasting ground. If we reverse our vision of the image and see the ground as the figure, the vase disappears and what emerges are two faces looking at one another. The dominance of one form has yielded to another.

Cartoons are drawings that define an object with lines

ABOVE. *It is easy to see why the white flowers are called gooseneck loosestrife (*Lysimachia clethroides*), as they poke their birdlike heads up to look around. The personality of the astilbes, with their crestfallen pink plumes, is less ebullient and more introspective. The photo was taken at the garden of Mr. and Mrs. Don Hewitt in the Hamptons on Long Island, New York.*

OPPOSITE. *The personalities of plants can complement one another, as illustrated by the tumbling, vining Lady Banks rose (*Rosa banksiae*) and the upright, arching stems of catmint (*Hepeta mussinii*). Wisteria blooms in the background at Ilmington Manor, near Avon, England.*

PAGES 58-59. *The tree trunk, its branches, the walkways, the house—almost all the elements that make up this picture are strongly linear, leading the eye in a twist back to the doorway of the house. The flowers are mere decoration. The garden is that of Mr. and Mrs. Andrew Norton at East Lambrook Manor near South Petherton, England, and once was the garden of Gertrude Jekyll.*

used as an outline. Cartoon artists circumscribe the object to make a pictograph of what it is, rather than produce an accurate drawing of its true appearance. Those who study classical drawing, on the other hand, learn to see how masses of light and shadow create forms, and how the lines describing boundaries thicken, thin, and sometimes disappear altogether as one makes one's way around the shape.

Similarly in the garden, masses of light and shadow create the overall forms in the landscape. The relative amounts of light and dark in the scene give us the essential information about the visual shapes to be found there. Placing a group of bushes and trees in a pleasing arrangement as individual forms is akin to outlining an object as a cartoon. A more accurate and subtle approach is needed if one wants to work with the forms that the eye actually sees.

Intellectually, we know that the shrubs are discrete plants, and so we may think of them that way. But thinking produces a mental idea of a thing, while seeing produces an actual image of the thing itself on the retina of the eye. When we look at a garden, we do not really see the shrubbery as a series of individual plants, but as masses of dark green against lighter backgrounds or light green against darker backgrounds. Even though, to the eye, shrubs in the border present a mottled appearance of varying shades of green, our first assessment of the whole border gives it a cohesive identity, so that we perceive the border as a figure against a ground.

TIPS FOR ASSESSING FORM

I have just gone outside and looked around my garden and beyond. The horizon is a nearby hill. I squinted at it so hard that the individual forms of things disappeared. I immediately saw that the hillside is made of two masses, one light—made up of the green grass—and the other dark, made up of conifers, deciduous trees, bushes, and bramble thickets. Then I opened my eyes and looked at these areas in detail. Both light and dark areas could be seen to be made of many different shades of green. In each, the mixture of masses gives a single predominant value to the area.

Then I started looking at smaller areas, such as the garden beds in my front yard, where there are dozens of trees, shrubs, vines, and herbaceous perennials. As I squinted at one garden area, plantings of about two dozen different plants resolved themselves into three different areas of light and dark. The lightest area was made up of sedum, sempervivum, echeverias, centaurea, stachys, and artemisia. The medium mass was comprised of perennials like sparaxis, *Ajuga,* agapanthus, nepeta, and veronica. And the darkest areas included pines, *Picea,* juniper, *Chamaecyparis,* and acanthus. To my satisfaction, even when all that could be discerned were three areas of light, medium, and dark, they fell together in a pleasing arrangement of five different shapes: two light areas separated by a dark

OPPOSITE TOP. *The garden resolves itself into light and dark masses no matter what the distance of the viewer from the feature. In the Pam Frost Garden in Vancouver, Canada, the viewer can take in a wide swathe of garden, with a bright fountain of tall oat grass (*Arrhenatherum elatius *'Variegatus') to the left of the black locust tree (*Robinia pseudoacacia*) balanced by the dark purple smoke bush (*Cotinus coggygria*) to the right. The backdrop of dark evergreens enhances the brighter yellow-gold plants in the foreground.*

OPPOSITE BOTTOM. *Repetition of forms and lines in the landscape pulls the picture together and gives it visual coherence. A masterful repetition of round forms is made at the Royal Botanic Garden in Edinburgh, Scotland, with the white plumey goats beard (*Aruncus dioicus*) in the background and the similarly shaped but much smaller* Astilbe *'Granat' in front. The astilbes are flanked by deep blue-purple* Iris sibirica *'Caesar' on the left and the paler species* Iris sibirica *on the right. The shape of these drifts of plants is shared by a stand of royal ferns (*Osmunda regalis *'Purpurescens') in the background, to the right of the goats beard. The limbs bursting from the top of the golden weeping willow (*Salix alba tristis*) add wonderfully energetic lines to the scene.*

RIGHT. *Besides visually strong or unique forms that are naturally inherent in the way plants grow, strong forms can be created by the gardener as well. The sculpted hedge of yew (*Taxus*) encloses a garden of mathematically precise beds bordered by the small-leaved boxwood (*Buxus microphylla *'Suffruticosa'). The white tulips keep the color scheme from interfering with the classical look of the scene, photographed at Madame Mallet's Garden at Parc des Moutiers in Varengeville-sur-mer in France.*

TOP. *The huge, coarse leaves of ornamental rhubarb (*Rheum palmatum*) give the plant a robust and powerful personality. The flowers of these plants are given a color-coordinated backdrop by the brick wall at Hadspen Garden, Somerset, England.*

ABOVE. *Good smells in the garden begin with the clean smell of woodsy leaf mold and sometimes, the roots that grow through it. The heart-shaped leaves belong to* Asarum canadense, *also known as wild ginger or Canadian snakeroot. When crushed, the root has a sweet, delicious, spicy smell. They are growing with cystopteris ferns at the C. Lindsay Smith Garden in Birmingham, Alabama.*

RIGHT. *A contrast of form is only emphasized by an added contrast in color. Light green maidenhair fern (*Adiantum capillus-veneris*) washes around a dark green, lustrous leaf of Lenten rose (*Helleborus orientalis*) at the Porter Carswell Garden in Savannah, Georgia.*

one, with two medium filling in around these.

When planning for harmonious form in the garden, you must first work with the masses of differing values. Then plan for color and textural and architectural effects. But first get the forms right. To do that, take an assessment of the plants in a nursery, in other people's plantings, or in nature by squinting at them and seeing how great an area of light or dark they create in relation to other plants around them. Remember that apparent masses of darkness and light can change. Daylily foliage may be medium next to gray-green iris swords, and light next to pine. In comparison to *Senecio cineraria,* daylily foliage might appear positively dark. The value of a plant can easily change with changes in context.

When placing plants in the garden, squint to see how the relative areas of light and dark look. If there is too much dark, extend the lighter area by using a plant with light green leaves. If you have too large a light area, use dark-leaved plants for balance.

Besides the overall forms of landscapes, beds, and borders and light and dark areas within them, there are the individual forms of plants. Iris, *Phormium,* and yucca all have stiff, upright, spiky, swordlike leaves. Yucca and *Phormium* leaves tend to

RIGHT. *Trees usually are the strongest forms in the landscape because of their bold shapes and sheer size. Close spacing causes these sycamores (*Platanus occidentalis*) to grow tall, straight, very impressive trunks that arch over a pathway at Versailles, France.*

TOP. *The color and form of the pretty hybrid* Phlox *'Chatahoochee' would contrast well with flowers like dark blue violet tulips.*

ABOVE. *White and purple forms of checkered fritillary (*Fritillaria meleagris*) bloom together at the Noble Garden in Sydney, Canada. The rare, incomprehensible checkering gives this plant a chimerical, even cartoonish, personality.*

TOP. *A striking form and color are combined in this orange-red flowering maple (*Abutilon pictum *'Thomsonii'), caught at perfection in the Volunteer Park Conservatory in Seattle, Washington.*

ABOVE. *Fringed oriental poppies (*Papaver orientale*) growing at Crathes Castle in Scotland also exemplify dramatic coloration and form.*

OPPOSITE. *A trio of dawn redwoods (*Metasequoia glyptostroboides*) are dressed in the soft colors of fall at the Berkeley Botanic Garden in Berkeley, California. These ancient trees will grow in perfectly regular conical shapes if given a spot by themselves in full sun.*

come from a small growing area at the base and ray outward, while iris forms enlarging clumps from which rows of swords arise. This kind of spiky form is very different from the soft, billowing masses of stems, leaves, and flowers of baby's breath (*Gypsophila paniculata*). When planted together, however, baby's breath and the coppery *Phormium tenax* balance each other perfectly.

It is great fun to work with forms in the landscape, because every plant's form tells the story of its strategy for survival. All green plants depend on light for survival, and their appearance describes how they go about collecting it. Some plants go big: *Gunnera, Rodgersia, Rheum,* and *Fatsia* all produce huge leaves that soak up gallons of light, while slender grass blades sip lightly at the shafts of sunlight that penetrate through the leaves overhead. Some leaves are deeply lobed to allow the wind to pass through without damaging them, while others end in pointed tips to collect and dispose of rainwater.

In a dramatic example of the function of plant form, California coast redwoods produce huge fans of tiny needles that rise hundreds of feet in the air to comb the dependable afternoon fogs for microdrops of water. The needles then consolidate them and drop them as a *faux* rain to the forest floor far below— the plant world's equivalent of a whale's filamentous baleen.

One of the most pleasing aspects of ornamental vines is the way they display themselves on trellises. It is almost as if they had a knack for it— which, of course, they do, having

evolved with the ability to display themselves for maximum effect amid the competition. They twist and turn as they grow and climb, but always have their leaves opened in the maximum plane of light availability.

The figure of each species of plant is its identity, and we recognize the plants by their signature forms. Certain forms—such as round-headed trees like crape myrtle (*Lagerstroemia indica*), slender cylinders like *Juniperus virginiana* 'Skyrocket', the neat cones of *Thuja plicata*, bushy and compact *Taxus*, and amorphous-shaped shrubs like philadelphus—benefit by contrast. You can help them stand out and be perceived separately by planting them with their opposites: place the slender trilon of *Juniperus* 'Skyrocket' next to the puffy perisphere of *Taxus baccata* 'Adpressus'. Both of these dark-leaved plants would flow together in an indistinguishable mass if they were the same shape, but their contrasting forms help keep them separate and add interest to the dark mass they form together in the landscape.

Flower forms are worth noticing and planning for in the garden. Again, look for contrast in form and color as the basic way of combining them. Try the broad, generous, purple-red flowers of a hybrid clematis ('Mme. Edouard André', for instance) climbing among the little pink double flowers of *Rosa polyantha* 'The Fairy'.

It can also be interesting to combine plants with the same flower form but with colors that are very different, or plants with flowers of the same color but with different

forms. In addition to seeking harmony of color combinations, work to balance contrasting forms to add interest and liveliness.

Some plants incorporate balance and contrast in and of themselves. The sinuous tendrils of the grapevine, for example, set off its pretty leaves and its inviting clusters of fruit. There is not much reason to try to combine these internal forms between plants. It makes little sense to plant two vines with similar tendrils together. These internal features are just characteristic of the plants and should be enjoyed for what they are.

TOP LEFT. *Cloudlike baby's breath* (Gypsophila paniculata) *is enthusiastic only about whatever it is planted with, never about itself. Here, associated with dominant and charismatic lilies, it is positively rapturous.*

BOTTOM LEFT. *Sometimes the most beautiful combinations of lights and darks as sheer forms occur as if by chance in the garden. Here in a private garden on Long Island, water gives a mottled light-and-dark background to an illuminated water lily* (Nymphaea) *in full bloom, while bayberry* (Myrica pensylvanica) *sprays its waxy-white fruits above.*

OPPOSITE. *Winter gives us a black-and-white snapshot of the permanent structure of our gardens, and with the landscape reduced to its simplest shapes, we can more easily tell whether we have the forms right. The midwinter snow reveals the interesting shape of the nicely pruned crab apples at Wayside Gardens, Creston, Canada, and emphasizes the importance of the softly curving handrail on the footbridge.*

*L*INE: THE DEFINING EDGE

Line is formed by the edges of an object, or by the narrow mass of a slender object. In the garden, line is seen in the tortuous curves of a tree branch, in the drape of a dormant vine over a doorway, or along the edge between the flower border and the lawn.

In designing a garden, it is important to work for interesting lines. Gardeners are frequently advised to plant some larger shrubs or perennials at the edge of a border so they spill out onto the grass. In this way, the line between the border and the lawn will wave and wiggle around the plants, breaking up the line and avoiding a dull, straight, decorative edge.

A strong line is found in the limbs of trees and woody shrubs, especially when these plants are silhouetted by light foliage behind them or by the sky. One of the most effective ways to see this kind of line is by standing in shadow under the closed canopy of a woods, looking through exposed limbs toward a sunny area beyond. The strong contrast makes the limbs stand out. When making a path through a shady part of the garden, look for interesting limbs. Is there already sunlight there? If not, can the background be cleared to allow sunlight to silhouette the limbs?

Besides these "found" objects—limbs already exposed—you can prune for good limbs. In fact, looking for beautiful limbs to expose on both woody shrubs and

ABOVE. *Nothing is simpler—yet more beautiful—than the curved line and refreshing flowers of* Clematis montana *'Rubrum' growing along a wall at the garden of Madame d'Andlau in Remalard, France.*

OPPOSITE. *Madrones (*Arbutus menziesii*) arch over a stone pathway at the Garden at Elk Rock in Portland, Oregon, creating a strong linear pattern that engages the eye and sweeps it off into the treetops.*

trees is a fascinating garden pastime. You can liken the task to Michelangelo's block of marble: the artist's job is to chip away everything extraneous, exposing the beauty that is already there.

Some plants are known for the beauty of their limbs and strong line quality and selected for planting with that purpose in mind. One such is *Magnolia soulangiana;* another is the wonderful New Zealand tea tree (*Leptospermum*); the *Amelanchier* and dogwood (*Cornus florida*) of the East; and the commercially available manzanitas of the West. Any of these might make a fine specimen planted in front of a smoke tree (*Cotinus coggygria*) in a spot that receives direct sun at some time in the day. In such an arrangement, the carefully pruned shrub or small tree in the foreground is able to display its beautiful limbs in front of, and somewhat mixed into, the powdery midsummer explosion of the smoke tree.

Morning or afternoon sun, noon sun only, or sun all day—your site determines the sun patterns. If you want to do as little work as possible, choose plants that fit your sun pattern, rather than trying to rearrange the landscaping to fit the plant selections. A spot that receives morning sunlight only might suit the dogwood. A spot in the hot, drying afternoon sun might displease a dogwood, but the New Zealand tea tree would love it.

To release limbs with strong, artful structure from the mishmash of limbs produced when a plant is left alone, wait until the plant is dormant, or—if it is an evergreen—

prune it in early summer. Prune cautiously, using a three-year schedule to get you where you want to go. Evergreens resent pruning more than deciduous plants; do extensive work in stages in early summer if you want to maintain a tree's shape, or when the plants are slowed for the winter if you want to revamp its look completely.

Before cutting, look carefully at the structure of the limbs and choose the one you think is most artfully formed. (It should be relatively mature.) Visualize that limb with its awkward shoots and side branches removed. Look for the core structure of the main branch—that is, the main thrust of the branch's growth.

You could, however, decide to release limbs that are less sculptural and more stately and dignified, or you could find a playful pattern to release. The choice is up to the gardener, but I think the most successful results occur when the limbs provide a bold, twisting, outward movement from the calm, center trunk.

When you have chosen this first limb, select another two or more to accompany it: these may balance it on the other side of the trunk, or run along with it on the same side. In either case, select these other limbs for their relationship to the first limb and their ability to harmonize with it visually. After you have decided which limbs are keepers, prune away the other lower limbs that hide them. In the case of a short plant, you may only need to take out limbs a few feet from the ground; if you are working with a mature tree, you may need to prune limbs above your

head. (In that event, *be sure* to consult a professional, for safety's sake.) You can leave areas of low foliage mixed with areas pruned open, so that as you walk along, the structural limbs are hidden, then revealed, then hidden again.

An especially artful way to prune is to reveal only a portion of a strong limb. Remove foliage selectively so that a part of a strong branch is seen within. This is an excellent technique to use with old rhododendrons, small azaleas, lilacs, *Spiraea, Corylus, Pittosporum,* and many other shrubs and small trees that present a bushy appearance.

There is usually so much bushiness in a garden that line quality is extremely important, first to vary the picture and relieve the look of lots of mounded puffs of shrubbery, and second to give a sense of the structure of the garden, of its skeleton, so to speak.

Strong structural lines in a garden should be revealed to suggest a deep, simple structure. Think of a flower arrangement in which beautiful curving, twisting twigs are used to indicate outward thrusting movements, while the flowers give substance and color. These twigs are usually placed so that they suggest a common source or center from which they originate. Picture where the common source of the limbs in your shrub patch might lie, then prune to reveal limbs that seem to originate from it. (This technique is effective even if this is all an artifice and there is no such center.) Doing so will make your landscape passage much more comprehensible and give it a satisfying look of unity.

RIGHT. *The trunks of old trees, like these ancient oaks in Beacon Hill Park, Victoria, Canada, create bold and thick lines in a landscape. Despite the daffodils' fresh spring song, the somnolent oaks have yet to begin to wake from their winter dormancy.*

BELOW. *Weeping Higan cherries (*Prunus subhirtella *'Pendula') are beautiful not only for their fountains of delicate, pink flowers, but also for the sight of the strong lines of their limbs flexing their muscles within clouds of color.*

ABOVE. *Sculpture gives focus and linear definition to leafy gardens that would otherwise be soft and undefined. In this private garden in Birmingham, Alabama, a sculpted figure brings the tight lines of a tense repose to the soft masses of azaleas behind it.*

ENHANCING FORM AND LINE

Another way to unify a planting is to repeat forms in the landscape. A large, rounded shape, for instance, when used in several places, pulls the scene together. Avoid the temptation to space repeated shapes at regular intervals. This gives a decorative staccato, rather than the pleasing asymmetry of forms that displays rhythm, variability, and punctuation.

You cannot only repeat forms, but turn them and twist them and use them in mirror-image fashion. For example, an upright, flat-topped, urn-shaped plant, such as a well-shaped Taxus, can be artfully arranged with a domed cedar—essentially the same shape turned upside down.

The outline of an irregularly shaped pool of water can be echoed in the shape of a bed of spring flowering bulbs nearby. Try placing benches of similar shape back to back some distance apart, creating a symmetry that can be interrupted by the dynamic forms of the plants between. Even in small parts of the garden, you can use the shapes that are there to please the aesthetic sense: the upturned cups of tulips placed with the downward bells of fritillaries, campanula, or hellebore, for instance, or a mat of busy little *Mazus reptans*—a tiny groundcover with miniature, light lavender to blue flowers dotted with white, yellow, and purple spots—in exactly the shape of a small compact mugho pine nearby.

I prefer to rely on a garden's resources rather than to introduce strictly decorative elements. Regarding garden statuary, my personal rule is that unless a piece of garden art is perfect in its place, forget it. When you want to include a piece of art, look at its form, rather than its content, to integrate it with the harmony of color, form, and line of your plants.

Seeing form in the landscape involves seeing shape without regard to its content—to see what is there, but not to identify it. This is pure visual seeing, unaffected by meaning or value. Recognize the beauty in the form, and then when meaning rushes back in, value will be enhanced. For example, I once noticed that the form of the *Acer palmatum* var. *dissectum* (the filigree-leaved Japanese maple) in my front garden looked like a birdbath. Not long afterwards, I came across a stone birdbath on a pedestal that had a shape very much like my maple's, so I bought it. When it was installed under the high side of the maple, the shapes and colors were wonderful together, although at first I chuckled at such similarity between two such different things. After a while, birds began to play and bathe in the water, using the maple tree above as their perch for drying. They were a lovely sight, preening themselves among the maple leaves and branches, fluttering down for a bath and then up again. Look at the shapes first, then the meanings of the shapes, and extra value follows.

Consider the form of the terrain in your garden. Is your property flat, or does it have slopes and hollows,

ABOVE. *The intriguing old jars at right and the terra cotta pots at left add visual interest to what might otherwise be an unremarkable terrace at the Netters garden in Long Island. Spaces have been left in the paving for thyme and lavender to grow.*

little hills and valleys, and jutting, craggy rocks? If your property has special features, you can use them as part of your design. If your property is flat, you may wish to hire a backhoe operator to create variations, cutting into the earth to make valleys and mounding up the excavated soil to make berms or little hills.

Water defines the shape of a garden's lowest spots because it will run and pond there. The tops of berms and slopes define the high places. Landscaping should work against the low spots and with the high spots. In other words, a tall, straight tree planted at the top of a hill will look like a carrot growing from the top of a raised bed. Plant it instead as a strong vertical in a low spot, working against the strong horizontal of ponding water. The vegetation on a hilltop should conform to the shape of the hill, and not confound it. Plant a field of wildflowers there to capture the sunlight, producing color in gaudy profusion. Plant bushy shrubs that will not interrupt the flow of the curve of the high land. Keep the planting low enough and open enough to provide a vista, and make the shelter in the low places. There plant the cathedral trees and the wet groundcovers and the subtle shady herbs like goldenseal.

In any garden, rock placement is important, for the rocks are the bones of a place. Artists working in pencil or charcoal often begin depicting the human form by drawing the bones, then the muscles, then the skin, finally erasing any trace of bone and muscle to result in an accurate, graceful drawing. Similarly, the landscape and garden designer needs first to arrange the rocks, then flesh out the rocks with soil; then artfully clothe this body in trees, shrubs, and herbaceous plants, perhaps leaving areas of rock and bare soil devoid of plant life. (Where you wish to keep the soil bare, cover it with pads of newspaper and a mulch of stones or sand or shredded bark. Avoid plastic mulch in permanent locations, as it eventually gets brittle and breaks up under the soil, and forever afterward you will be picking annoying and ugly shreds of plastic from your beautiful garden soil.)

OPPOSITE TOP. *Purple aubrieta and pink and white helianthemum are gauzy plants that serve to soften the hard edges of stone steps. The urn shape of the brown Chinese pot is repeated several times in this scene in the shape of the rounded mounds of herbs and shrubs, but turned upside down. The photograph was taken at a private garden in the village of Crewkerne, England.*

OPPOSITE BOTTOM. *When all the formal design elements of the garden—line, form, color, composition—and all the romantic elements—atmosphere, season, light quality—come together into a coherent whole, our dreams come to soft, green life. An example is the garden of Madame d'Andlau in Remalard, France, resolving itself out of the early morning mist.*

RIGHT. *To decorate this wall in a private garden in Chipping Camden, England, the gardener chose a simple arrangement of three familiar plants—coral bells (*Heuchera), *campanula, and a rose. Despite the simplicity of the design—or perhaps because of it—they create a visually rich picture.*

MAKING A GARDEN COMPOSITION

Dealing with form in the garden requires simplicity. Too many different kinds of forms make a busy hodgepodge. Two, or at most three forms should be used to build a pleasing garden composition.

The most stable and pleasing garden compositions are based on a triangle, with its broad base at the bottom and its top point somewhat off-center to achieve asymmetricality. (A symmetrical composition usually lacks dynamism.)

The strong verticals of upthrusting stones, for instance, may be one type of form to use in building the triangle. Strong verticality can be repeated by other nearby rocks. Thus the rocks might build to a crescendo, with the most dramatic rock at the apex of the compositional triangle. Balance this dramatic rock with less dramatic but larger ones placed nearby for balance. Other verticals that echo the stones can be given by the straight trunks of trees, an upright shrub, or garden buildings or furniture.

A second form may be low and rounded and very rooted to the earth on which it lies. It can be created by rounded rocks like cabochons; rounded berms or small hills covered with grass, moss, or a low groundcover; green shrubs with rounded forms mixed with rounded yellow- or burgundy-leaved shrubs, and rounded trees.

Some compositions involve all rounded shapes, relieved by just one or two very strong vertical shapes. These can be worked into the composition or you can use your rounded shapes in a composition made up chiefly of verticals.

If a third form seems to be needed, you can integrate something as simple as the shape of a pool of water, delineated by a sinuous line that subtly echoes the rounded forms of the rocks, trees, and shrubs. If water is not a possibility, gravel or stones can be substituted. Depending on their color, they can blend into the

OPPOSITE TOP. *The dominant landscape elements in this view of the garden of Mr. and Mrs. W. Irving at Greencroft House, Great Strickland, England, are those with the strongest line quality: the circular pool of water edged with stones and the huge parabola of the evergreen in the background heaving out of sight. All the shapes carry the eye to the perfectly placed immensity of the* Gunnera manicata *at the back end of the pool.*

OPPOSITE BOTTOM. *Very formal, symmetrical composition characterizes this garden at Lawhead Croft in Scotland. The formality produces a strong perspective that whisks the eye right out of the garden to the meadows and woods beyond.*

RIGHT. *The sinuous lines of sculpted birds adorn a bed of* Salvia x superba *at Peter Newton's garden in Saint Helena, California. Without the strong movement of the sculpture, this garden would have far less interest and drama. With it, the scene turns positively theatrical.*

PAGES 78-79. *Stones add new colors to relieve too much green along a pond shore in the garden of Mrs. J. H. Robinson and Mr. John Brookes at Denmans, England. A statue called* The Dreamer *infuses the scene with a feeling of quiet transport.*

landscape or be very visible, making a strong line when bordered by green grass. These areas of stone can be made into a level pool that suggests water remarkably well.

Paths make strong linear statements in the garden, saying to us: walk here. They are the final element in the composition. Our eyes are pulled to them and along them. Paths are more interesting if they meander, taking a person toward interesting features as one progresses through the garden.

Simplicity produces feelings of tranquility and repose. These feelings are not spiritless, far from it. In simple, effective gardens, nature's silent energy is awesomely present. Simplicity allows for stillness; only in the stillness can we remove our clattering minds from the picture. In attempting to do just one thing to perfection, all the other things on which it depends must be done well, too, and so the garden falls into place around a simple idea.

A simple idea might be to create a cascade of plants, stones, and earth down a bank. If we think of the cascade as a basic form, we can make a simple arrangement of stones and earth and plants with appropriate shapes. Then we fine-tune by selecting plants with the shapes we want that also work in terms of leaf shape, color, texture, and other desirable characteristics.

LEFT. *Simplicity is as much a virtue in gardening as in any other art. In a private garden in Chipping Camden, England, an old-fashioned rose and a planting of* Helleborus foetidus *grace a stone wall. Though simple, the scene lacks nothing.*

THE GARDEN AS A WHOLE

Even though we use the concepts of light, color, lines, masses, and forms when designing, the eye appreciates the garden as a whole, and it is best to remember that. Anything that destroys the integral quality of the garden should be removed. If any element—a plant, statue, stone, or path—is awkward, disruptive, out of place, or clashes, be ruthless about changing it or getting rid of it. Make the garden a simple, whole, easy-to-understand place that communicates directly and quickly about its virtues and joys, without a million distractions.

Simplicity pleases the eye in a comprehensive way. The hard work of gardening vanishes, the thought and planning evaporate, and there it stands not as something a person has made, but as a place that is simply itself, being beautiful in the sublimely unself-conscious way of nature.

The best gardens are the most beautiful, and the most beautiful gardens are simple, their concept single-minded, and their execution focused and unscattered. Such gardens are invariably thought of as places where it would be good to spend some time, where it would be good to live and eat and drink and walk. There is a sense of truth about a great garden—an inevitability, as though this must be, even though no gardener had made it.

All this we perceive through our eyes. Confronted with the vision of a beautiful garden intelligently and artfully arranged, we see something

beautiful about ourselves, as part of nature. No wonder we encounter the vision of a beautiful garden with joy! It is a glimpse of nature perfected; it is a glimpse of the spirit within and without.

ABOVE. *Stones have strong linear outlines, and their placement in the landscape is important in giving a scene weight and structure. But sometimes, as with this bench and stone facing two huge Oregon white oaks* (Quercus garryana) *in the Garden at Elk Rock in Portland, Oregon, stone placement can be done on a small scale with a big dash of whimsy.*

Smell

*The breath of flowers is far sweeter
in the air (where it comes and goes like
the warbling of music) than in the hand.*
Francis Bacon

There comes a day in late winter or early spring when you can smell the earth again. Before the leaves or flowers emerge, the sun warms the winter-wracked earth, and from it arises the scent of what the winter has wrought: mats of dead leaves, the smell of raw soil, the duff on the forest floor, last year's detritus.

On such a day, it is time to poke into last fall's compost pile. Into the pile went leaves and old garden pullings, orange peels, manure from the farm, grass cuttings, and—if you are lucky enough to live by the water—seaweed. What magic winter has performed! Weeds and leaves and grasses and garbage have become rich, black, decayed, humusy compost—at once the source and destination of life.

Walt Whitman stood in awe of this process. In his poem, "This Compost," he wrote:

Now I am terrified at the Earth, it is that calm and patient.
It grows such sweet things out of corruption,
It turns harmless and stainless on its axis, with such endless
*   succession of diseas'd corpses,*
It distills such exquisite winds out of such infused fetor,
It renews with such unwitting looks its prodigal, annual,
*   sumptuous crops,*
It gives such divine materials to men, and accepts such
*   leavings from them at last.*

Compost breathes, taking in air that stokes the soil microbes to new life, breathing out the scent of that new life—the deep, bass smell of mushrooms and old moss, with just an oboe's hint of sweet violets and fresh rootlets. This is reminiscent of the ancient "ur" smell, from the secret place where seeds stir and new life begins.

This is the fragrance that greets us on that warming day early in the year, when we can finally smell the earth again. Today is such a day, and as I write this, my knees are wet and dirty from kneeling on the new earth, and the smell of the soil is fresh in my mind and on my hands.

Most of us can remember this smell from our early childhood. It is one of the most evocative in bringing to mind that far-off time, along with freshly mown grass, burning leaves in the fall, the electric zing of ozone in the air after a summer thundershower. Smells are strongly imprinted on our memories—so strongly that throughout our lives, a particular smell will trigger a memory of another time, jog us back there, and we will remember details that otherwise would have evaporated with the passage of the years.

Why is this so? Primarily, because mothers and infants recognize each other by smell. Before a baby learns to use its vision, he or she can find his or her mother; this is a talent we come equipped with. It is the first experience, to search for food by smell—to find the mother, then the nipple, and then the milk that means life itself.

This ability to search for food by smell carries on into adulthood. Envision the life led by our progenitors for several million years as our bodies developed. Until the invention of agriculture, just the blink of an eye ago, human beings were hunters and gatherers. There would be great survival value in remembering where we encountered the wild apples in bloom, or the dank place where the delicious yellow fungi sprouted, or the particular stretch of riverbank where the perfumy wild grapes hung thickest through the trees. As humans roamed the world seeking food, we would naturally remember those places and return there seasonally. These scents provided us with a memory map of our provender, much as wild animals recognize territories by scent. Without the ability to rely on our sense of smell, humans would have had to rely on pure luck and chance to find food. Thanks to a keen sense of smell, we remembered, we returned, we were sustained. Food smells tend to be unmistakable. Think of the

characteristic smells of vanilla, cinnamon, cloves, licorice, almonds, oregano, rosemary, mint, pineapple, strawberries, and bananas. These scents are instantly recognizable. The intensity tells us how safe or how ripe and ready to eat food is. (Flower scents, on the other hand, tend to be subtle.)

The sense of smell is also one of the most personal. Few of us will come up with the same descriptors for a subtle smell. For many of us, the scent of flowers takes us back to our grandparents' gardens, with their hyacinths, lilacs, and roses. We ran through these gardens and smelled the fragrances that bonded us to the garden forever. How many of our own gardens now are recreations of those childhood memories and versions of the Edens we knew then? As Louise Beebe Wilder wrote in *The Fragrant Path*,

*Fragrance speaks more clearly to
    age than to youth.
With the young, it may not pass
    much beyond the
olfactory nerve, but with those who
    have started down
the far side of the hill it reaches into
    the heart.*

Think of the delicate and evasive scents of irises, wisteria, stock, dianthus, and even apple blossoms. We do not eat these; their scents are an aesthetic experience rather than a matter of survival. These subtle scents charm us with their elegance. Their very elusive and undefinable qualities enchant us as we seek to capture them in our memories. They call to us, tease us, lead us on with

ABOVE. *It is on just such a day as this one at Showskill Manor, Broadway, England, that the smell of the soil and rain, stones and flowers returns with its friendly earthy perfume. Clumps of red valerian* (Centranthus ruber), *low mounds of thyme, and an ornamental grapevine relish the misty wet day.*

OPPOSITE. *On a warming day in spring, we realize with surprise that we can again smell the earth—such as the truffly smell of these decaying hawthorn* (Crataegus) *leaves and fruits at the Finch Arboretum in Spokane, Washington.*

PAGES 82-83. *The snow of ornamental cherry blossoms has a light scent of pollen that by sheer virtue of their numbers can fill the air around the tree. This specimen is growing above a bed of* Bergenia cordifolia *at Denmans, England, a garden designed by Mrs. J. H. Robinson and Mr. John Brookes. No blossoms have a nicer scent than apples—my personal favorite flower scent.*

ABOVE. *When an iris opens its golden throat, like this one at the Pam Frost garden in Vancouver, British Columbia, its breath is as refreshing to the nose as a spring rain. This iris is associating with* Saxifraga umbrosa *'Variegata.'*

OPPOSITE TOP. *The scent of roses dominates this private garden in Santa Barbara, California, at least until the lemon tree blooms. Of all garden flowers, citrus blossoms may project their scent the farthest—even to a hundred yards away if the wind is just right. Spanish lavender* (Lavandula stoechas) *adds a grace note to this bouquet.*

OPPOSITE BOTTOM. Campanula persicifolia's *cheery bells ring out the news that the rose is opening and its scent is beginning to spill out. Red roses tend to have more scent than lighter-colored ones. This combination is growing in the garden of the Marquess and Marchioness of Salisbury at Hatfield House, Hatfield, England.*

their whispered sweet nothings. They do not direct us to a food, to a flavor, and they are not completely engulfed and understood the way food smells are. They are for the nose only. In a world of "off" smells, bad smells, and downright disgusting smells, the fragrances of the garden are balm for the nose.

The scent of flowers is best encountered by chance, as when you are standing on a veranda and suddenly become aware of the sweet scent of honeysuckle. We gardeners know where our scented flowers are tucked, but visitors are often aware of the perfume before they discover its source.

Some scented flowers are star performers in the garden, not tucked away anywhere, but planted out for all to see. Fragrant roses come to mind. Other heavily fragrant plants, like star jasmine (*Trachelospermum jasminoides*), may be hardly noticeable in the mix of the landscaping until their aromas come to us, and we search the shrubbery with our eyes, looking for the profuse flushes of little pink and white stars. It is great fun to hide fragrant plants where visitors will be sure to smell them without seeing them, and then to watch them snoop around the plantings, nose-first. To do this, choose plants that project their aromas over some distance.

We can classify flowers by how far they project their scent. Delicate rose fragrances may not be perceptible until the nose is perched, bee-like, on the tuft of yellow stamens in the center of the flower. The sharp, clean smell of rosemary in full sun may be noticeable from several feet away but no farther. And yet even a small *Daphne odora* will set its scent sailing on the wind, and you can pick it up all the way across the yard.

Plants that project their scents for distances are casting a wide net for pollinating insects, and they do this by means of volatile fatty acids, or oils, that evaporate, carrying the delicate molecules of scent with them into the air. Our olfactory cells—two nerve-rich spots on the roof of the upper nasal passage—are very much like velcro, on a molecular level. When a molecule of scent arrives, it has a configuration that makes it stick to the nerve, creating in our consciousness a certain impression of the scent. Varying scent molecules lock into the nerves in different ways, creating the almost infinite variety of scents that we can distinguish. The presence of large quantities of volatile oil can be seen in the gas plant (*Dictamnus albus*), a taprooted garden perennial. For years I had heard that the gas plant emitted a vapor that could be lit, just like a gas burner. So one day I headed for the garden with matches in hand to see if the rumor was true. There was no such flammable "breath" from the opened flowers, but below these were half-opened flower buds that formed little chambers. When I touched a flame to the hole in the end of the chamber, it lit and sent out a tiny tongue of fire. Evidently, as the flowers open, the citrusy-smelling volatile oil produced in the flower is trapped in these chambers at concentrated, flammable levels. As the petals separate and open, the vapor is more easily dissipated.

Another way that we classify fragrances is by how much we like them. Just about everyone loves the honey-and-spice sweetness of a Korean spice viburnum (*Viburnum carlesii*), and we can all agree on the really bad odors without reciting their names. Then there are those in the middle: some people just love the pungent fragrance of night-blooming jasmine (*Cestrum nocturnum*), while others think it far too heavy and cloying. Like patchouli, one either loves it or despises it, but it is too strong to ignore.

We can also classify flower scents according to the type of smells they are: spicy, sweet, citrusy, and so forth. Among the Mediterranean herbs, especially, it is easy to detect relationships; these plants produce volatile oils that are clearly similar in aroma. They include thyme, sage, lavender, rosemary, and the *Artemisia*s, such as wormwood and southernwood. You can add to this group plants like mint and catnip.

Belladonna lily (*Amaryllis belladonna*), also known as naked lady, in the fall produces bright pink flowers with a heavy, sickly, cloying scent. Several other very fragrant plants, like the *Cestrum nocturnum* (mentioned above), star jasmine (*Trachelospermum jasminoides*), jasmine (*Jasminum* x *grandiflorum*), gardenias, and jonquils, also carry a heavy scent that is best encountered attenuated upon the air.

Spicy-scented flowers include the clove-scented *Viburnum carlesii*, dianthus species, the licorice-scented hyssop, Arabian jasmine (*Jasminum sambac*), and others with scents that tend toward incense.

The smell of honey hangs heavy in fields full of wild bergamot, also known as Oswego tea (*Monarda fistulosa*), a native wildflower of the eastern United States that turns whole meadows rosy lavender in the summer. Honey aromas run from the dry, musty smell of *Photinia fraseri* to the slightly almondlike smell of the flowers of English hawthorn (*Crataegus laevigata*); from the honey-and-lemon scent of lemon verbena leaves to the musky honey smell of the musk roses (*Rosa moschata*).

Some smells can only be described as sweet: new-mown hay, for instance, many of the lilies, clover blossoms, the rampant Japanese honeysuckle (*Lonicera japonica*), *Daphne odora, Crinum,* and violets.

Roses have a unique fragrance, familiar from attar of roses or scented rosewater, that varies from fruity through musky, according to the type of rose. Some people consider the scent of the damask rose, (*Rosa damascena*) as the "true" rose scent, although others would argue for *Rosa gallica,* the old French rose. The choice of the truest rose scent is subjective, of course, but both damask roses and French roses have been around for centuries and have been used extensively, especially in Bulgaria, to make the very attar that characterizes the scent of rose in our minds. Damask roses are also known as autumnal roses, or "roses of four seasons," because they bloom from summer into early autumn. Some hybrids, like 'Ispahan', have an extremely long blooming season. A Mediterranean species, *Rosa damascena semperflorens,* is believed to have been grown at Pompeii; Virgil describes a similar fragrant rose that blooms twice a year. We cannot leave the subject of damask roses without a word of praise for this group, which produces rather unimportant-looking semidouble flowers and a fragrance that recalls a thousand years full of starry nights and all the sweet romances that played out their dramas beneath them. The damask cultivar named 'Madame Hardy', a white rose, has a greater power to project its scent than most of the other damasks. For the more floral scent in roses, go for the grandiflora 'Queen Elizabeth', or perhaps the climbing sport of 'Don Juan'.

Many other plants have unique smells that are less usefully characterized. The big, citrusy-smelling blossoms of *Magnolia grandiflora* have a tropical note. And how can one characterize the softly sweet fragrance of lily of the valley (*Convallaria majalis*), except to say that it occurred in powder form in a round box on mother's vanity?

Wisteria has a distinctive smell, as does the similarly scented lilac (*Syringa vulgaris*). The latter has given its name to its scent, as have lavender, rose, and violet. All of them are also the names of their characteristic colors, revealing how these plants appeal to several senses at once, providing pleasure to them all individually in a grand synthesis.

ABOVE. *The beautiful powdery blue fruit of leatherleaf mahonia* (Mahonia bealei) *look like they would smell of grapes, but their scent is only slightly fruity.*

OPPOSITE TOP. *Waves of crabapple blossoms spray their light floral scent onto passersby at the Cummins Garden in Portland, Oregon.*

OPPOSITE BOTTOM. *Wisteria is a plant whose flowers will project their scent over distances. As we perambulate this path through the garden of C. Lindsay Smith in Birmingham, Alabama, looking at the colors of the tulips, light lavender stars of* Phlox divaricata, *and the blue-green grassy leaves of ophiopogon edging the path, we will be pleased by the fragrance of* Wisteria sinensis 'Alba' *the whole way along.*

PLANNING FRAGRANCES ACCORDING TO SEASON

Still another way to characterize fragrant plants is by the time of year that they bloom. This information is useful in selecting plants with overlapping bloom times so that there is always something perfuming the air.

Among the trees, there is something fragrant blooming in every season. In winter, the witch hazels bloom. The native witch hazel (*Hamamelis virginiana*) unfurls its long, ribbonlike petals in late fall to early winter, and they produce a sweet scent. But for fragrance, plant a specimen of *Hamamelis mollis,* the Chinese witch hazel, which blooms in February to March with yellowish ribbons and a strong, pure, clear fragrance akin to that of jonquils. On cold days, the ribbons roll up, waiting for warm weather to unfurl again.

Also open in February and sometimes into March is the aptly named winter sweet, a small tree or large woody shrub. It opens yellowish brown, usually downward-facing cups held tightly to the woody branches. The scent of this tree on a warm late February day is enchanting, coming as it does when little else is on the air. The fragrance is spicy, sweet, almost like jasmine, and it carries far.

From April to August, *Magnolia grandiflora* opens its huge, waxy, white blossoms from Maryland to the Gulf of Mexico and along the Pacific Coast. They carry a volatile, sweet, citrus-candy scent. Two other magnolias are well-known for their fragrance; my favorite is *Magnolia stellata*, the star magnolia. In April its bare branches are graced with myriad three-inch (7.6 cm) fragrant white stars. Probably the most fragrant magnolia of all is the large Yulan Magnolia (*Magnolia heptapeta*), which produces three-inch (7.6 cm), chalice-shaped white flowers in April.

From mid-April to May, the flowering crab apples bloom, drowning themselves in sweet flowers, most of which have a striking apple-blossom scent. Of all the floral fragrances in the plant kingdom, can anything touch the sweetness of apple blossoms? Barely a pink whisper of the scent, and yet so enticing, fresh, and clean.

In June the sourwood (*Oxydendrum arboreum*) opens its hanging panicles of fragrant, white, bell-shaped florets. It is a native of the Southeast and does best there. Another June bloomer is the seldom-planted but beautiful epaulette tree (*Pterostyrax hispidus*). Hardy to Zone 5, it produces creamy white, fragrant, puffy flowers that hang in braided panicles said to resemble the epaulettes of a military uniform.

Also hardy, this to Zone 6, is fragrant snowbell (*Styrax obassia*), which blooms from May to June with racemes of three-quarter-inch (1.9 cm) white florets, and a far-carrying scent.

Yellowwood (*Cladrastis lutea*) only blooms in June every few years, so you cannot always count on a floral show. When it does bloom, it produces profusions of hanging clusters of white, pealike, strongly fragrant flowers, perfuming the air around it.

In July, no tree works better between a woods and a lawn than a gorgeous specimen of goldenrain tree (*Koelreuteria paniculata*). Its very showy, foot-tall, upright clusters of soft, yellow flowers carry a sweet floral essence.

The waxy, white flowers of the Franklin tree (*Franklinia alatamaha*) appear in August to September and are lightly fragrant.

Among the shrubs, the year starts early with the daphnes; *Daphne odora* throws its fragrance across the entire yard and has been called the most strongly perfumed of all the plants. It blooms in March. In late March, *Daphne mezereum* blooms with a lilac scent that can perfume the entire property. Fragrant guelder, or *Viburnum fragrans*, blooms all winter in mild areas, and in March in the Northeast, where its lilac scent is much appreciated in the bare months.

The leatherleaf mahonia (*Mahonia bealei*) bursts into yellow bloom in March as far north as Zone 6 and continues blooming into April. Its flower buds hang like strings of beads and are quite strongly scented when they open above the prickly, thick, evergreen leaves. A good companion is the sweet box, *Sarcococca humilis* or *S. hookeriana*. Its pinkish flowers are small and inconspicuous, but they will strongly perfume the air with a sweet, honeyed scent in late winter.

Under this early, fragrant bloom, the young violets are blooming—especially *Viola odorata*. One must get down on one's hands and knees

to smell these pretty little flowers, but the effort is worth it.

In Zone 9, you can plant *Choisia ternata,* the Mexican orange, which carries sprays of white flowers with an orange-blossom scent in March and April.

A March–April bloomer in areas to Zone 6 is the buttercup winter hazel (*Corylopsis pauciflora*). This little treasure has fragrant, yellow, bell-shaped flowers in clusters of two or three, hanging from its still-bare branches.

Among shrubs, a blooming season from March to May is unusual, but drooping leucothoe (*Leucothoe fontanesiana*), the evergreen with the racemes of fragrant, lily-of-the-valley–shaped flowers that hang under the leaves over this long period.

Cold-area gardeners will like the Nanking cherry (*Prunus tomentosa*), which is hardy to Zone 2. In April it bursts into sweetly fragrant, pinkish white bloom, followed by edible red cherries from June into July.

In Zones 8 to 10, gardeners can plant *Pittosporum tobira,* the Japanese pittosporum, which develops clusters of whitish yellow flowers at the branch tips from April to May. The clusters emit a fragrance like light orange or lemon blossoms, but this scent is not projected far from the plant.

The clove currant, *Ribes odoratum,* is a good choice for a special fragrance treat in the spring. The bush grows to about six feet tall (1.8 meters), but widens to eight feet (2.4 meters) across with age. In April to May it produces yellow and red tubular flowers that hang in groups of five to ten blossoms on a raceme and produce a spicy, sweet scent reminiscent of cloves.

In April and May, the *Daphne cneorum,* or garland daphne, produces tightly packed clusters of fragrant, rose-pink florets at the branch ends. It is a small plant, evergreen, and short enough to qualify as a ground cover.

In April and May come the heavily scented blossoms of the fragrant viburnums—*Viburnum carlesii, V.* x *burkwoodii, V.* x *carlecephalum,* and *V.* x *juddii.* The latter is the least fragrant of the group. Known as spice viburnum, *V. carlesii* has a distinctly spicy, clovelike scent that hangs heavy in the spring air.

The lovely tree peony (*Paeonia suffruticosa*) opens its silky petals in May. The double blooms are big, from six to twelve inches (15.2 to 30.4 cm) across. They carry the typical peony fragrance. Many shades of red, pink, yellow, and white are available.

May is also the month for the lilacs, both *Syringa* x *chinensis,* the Chinese lilac, and *Syringa vulgaris,* the French lilac. Both types of lilac have many cultivars in many color variations of lilac, lavender, white, purple, and reddish purple. The chief difference between them is that the Chinese lilac is shorter and finer looking, with a billowing effect to the plant. Both have the distinctive and beautiful lilac scent.

From late May into June, the mock orange (*Philadelphus coronarius*) bursts into exuberant bloom, covering itself with pure white, fresh, clean flowers that smell of citrus, jasmine, and orange blossoms. Carolina allspice (*Calycanthus floridus*) is commonly sold for its sweet, spicy, juicyfruit-scented, reddish brown flowers that appear in May and June. Nurserypeople have warned me that some clones have no scent or a positively "off" scent. So if you try this plant, make sure to buy a specimen with the sweet scent for which it is named.

From May to November, the

prized *Gardenia jasminoides* opens its waxy, white, single-rose–type blossoms with the familiar and heavy gardenia smell. The plant is evergreen, stays small and compact, and is finicky. It grows well only where it likes its spot and has moist, humusy, acidic soil. Hardy outside only to Zone 8, the gardenia is familiar in pots in the colder zones. A June-blooming daphne is the hybrid *Daphne* x *burkwoodii,* with very fragrant clusters of white flowers.

July brings the buddleias into bloom, especially the honey-scented purple panicles of *Buddleia davidii,* the butterfly bush. This plant is so named because butterflies cannot resist its florets, which form long, pointed clusters at the tips of arching branches. Buddleia is one of the best and most beautiful plants in any garden. In addition to this species, *Buddleia alternifolia* has prettily scented, lilac-colored flowers that flock its long stems in June, forming a fountain of flowers.

One of the latest-blooming shrubs—or small tree, if pruned to a standard—is the sweet pepperbush, also called summer sweet (*Clethra alnifolia*). It has many advantages, being hardy to Zone 3, staying just eight to ten feet tall (2.4 to 3 meters) and four to five feet (1.2 to 1.5 meters) across, producing six-inch (15.2 cm) spikes of small white florets in August. This shrub is a welcome sight late in the year, and the flowers are fragrant. I especially like the pink cultivar, 'Pinkspire'; it associates nicely with the deep purple flowers of *Liriope muscari,* which can be planted under the tree and blooms at the same time.

VINES: FRAGRANCE ON THE MOVE

For some reason, many of the most startlingly fragrant plants are vines —the most little-used class of plants in the ornamental garden. Many vines are tender and cannot persist in the colder climates, but there are fragrant vines for every region.

One of the first to bloom is the Carolina yellow jessamine (*Gelsemium sempervirens*), hardy to Zone 7. In February, clusters of small, funnel-shaped flowers carry a fresh, sweet scent, with bloom extending into March.

Another February bloomer is pink jasmine (*Jasminum polyanthum*)—a wonderful plant but only hardy to Zones 9 and 10. It grows to be a big vine with lots of finely filigreed foliage and freely produced masses of small pink buds that open to heavily fragrant white flowers. This jasmine will perfume the air for many feet around it—it is one that you discover first with your nose.

When March arrives, the poet's jasmine (*Jasminum officinale*) welcomes the end of the winter with the scent we have come to associate with the word jasmine—rich, sweet, almost like incense. It continues to open flowers more sparingly through the summer and most of the fall.

The evergreen clematis (*Clematis armandii*) has long, pointed foliage that tends to get ratty in late winter, but then makes up for its appearance with a show of starlike flowers in March and April that reveal a pretty scent up close. It is hardy to Zone 7.

The warmest zones are the most graced by fragrant vines, such as the Easter-lily vine (*Beaumontia grandiflora*), hardy only to Zone 9. It gives a tropical effect, opening many big, fragrant trumpets from April to September. Also in April, the star jasmines (*Trachelospermum*) begin to bloom, continuing their bloom until July or August. First comes *T. asiaticum,* the yellow star jasmine, soon followed by the white blooms of star jasmine (*T. jasminoides*). The yellow species is not as vigorous as the white. Both have a jasmine scent, but the star jasmine's is particularly rich and heavy, very much like a true jasmine. Hardy to Zone 9, *T. jasminoides* will form a ground cover, or, if a support is within reach, it will climb. In California, star jasmine enwreathes porch posts. The yellow-flowered *T. asiaticum* is a little more hardy, to Zone 8.

OPPOSITE. *A mass of* Clematis montana *'Rubrum' climbs the chateau wall at the garden of Princess Sturdza at La Vasterival in Varengeville-sur-mer in France. Its amorphous form softens the hard edges of the building's structure.*

TOP. *For all its invasive faults, common honeysuckle (*Lonicera japonica*) throws a spicy, honeyed smell onto the late spring and early summer air. Here it is rather attractively burying a fence above plantings of dark purple salvia in the garden of Jim and Connie Cross in Cutchogue, New York*

RIGHT. *Wisteria grows around a window at a private garden in England. On a sunny morning, the home owner may throw open the window to invite the perfumed zephyrs into the house.*

ABOVE AND OPPOSITE. Clematis patens *'Nelly Moser' is among the most beloved and lovely of this genus, which includes the fragrant species* Clematis armandii *and* C. dioscoreifolia.

April also brings the wisterias. Japanese wisteria (*Wisteria floribunda*) produces long, fragrant clusters. A pair of cultivars, *W. f.* 'Longissima' (violet) and *W. f.* 'Longissima alba' (white), produces clusters up to three feet (91.4 cm) long. Probably the most fragrant is *W. f.* 'Rosea', with its fifteen- to eighteen-inch (38.1 to 45.7 cm) pink clusters lasting until May.

April and May are the months for the more familiar Chinese wisteria (*Wisteria sinensis*), with shorter clusters with a heady lilac fragrance that carries when released in full sun onto warm winds. Wisteria has been described as the perfect flowering plant—hardy to Zone 4, always beautiful of form, great fragrance, lovely color, never looks tired, will cover a whole wall—with only one drawback: too short a season of bloom.

Still another jasmine, the angel-wing jasmine (*Jasminum nitidum*), begins its bloom in May and continues in flushes of blossoms until August. Its starry, white blossoms look like elegant pinwheels settled on the shrubby vine's stiff branches. The smell is floral, fresh, sweet, and delicate. To sense it, you have to get your nose right up to the blossom.

Madagascar jasmine (*Stephanotis floribunda*) is a tropical vine that opens its waxy flowers in May and keeps them coming into October. In most places it is an indoor plant and well worth it, as the scent is rich, incense-like jasmine.

Then comes June and the fragrant vines are suddenly bursting out all over. In Zone 6 and warmer, the climbing hydrangea vine (*Decumaria barbara*) hangs fragrant, hydrangea-like white flowers above its glossy foliage. June and July are the season for the lovely evergreen waxflower (*Hoya carnosa*), found in pots everywhere but planted outside only in Zone 10, for it can stand no frost. The flowers are exceptional little five-pointed stars that look as though they are carved from white wax with a red center. The scent is honey-sweet.

In June the royal jasmine (*Jasminum grandiflorum*) blooms in Zone 7 and warmer. The shrubby vine produces flowers all summer, and their scent carries quite a distance.

Also in June come the honeysuckles, starting with the tropical (Zone 10) giant Burmese honeysuckle, *Lonicera hildebrandiana*. This large beauty opens six-inch (15.2 cm) flower tubes with a tropical honeysuckle fragrance. This is a good plant in a sunroom or greenhouse in the cold regions.

Two fragrant, hardy honeysuckles are the familiar Hall's honeysuckle (*Lonicera halliana*) and the woodbine honeysuckle (*L. periclymenum*). Both are hardy to Zone 4. Hall's is the familiar honeysuckle that runs rampant through the woods and hedgerows and old playgrounds of the Northeast. Familiar though it is, the fragrance is warm and sweet and pleasant, and carries many feet in the warm summer air.

Although it is hardy only to Zone 9, a word must be said about Chilean jasmine (*Mandevilla laxa*). This twining vine opens two-inch (5.1 cm), white, trumpet-shaped, and delicately formed flowers in clusters of five or six from June into August. The fragrance is a heavenly, floral perfume. I have grown one up my Gravenstein apple tree in the front yard, and when the apple blossoms are finished, the jasmine keeps the fragrance coming from the top of the tree, where it curls and cascades.

A fragrant passion vine, the hybrid passionflower (*Passiflora* x *alatocaerulea*), blooms from June to October in Zone 8 and warmer in shades of white and pink with a bluish purple crown. The passion-flowers are four inches (10.2 cm) across and nicely perfumed.

The Madeira vine (*Anredera cordifolia*) is a native of Paraguay, which accounts for its desire to delay bloom until August. It stays in bloom into October, with foot-long (30.5 cm) clusters of tiny, sweetly fragrant flowers.

The last of the vines to bloom is also one of the hardiest. The sweet autumn clematis (*Clematis paniculata*) is hardy to Zone 5 and produces profuse panicles of fragrant, inch-long (2.5 cm) flowers from September into October. It is evergreen in zones 8 and 9, deciduous in zones 5 through 7.

FRAGRANT PERENNIALS

Many gardeners, myself among them, favor herbaceous perennials in their gardens. The green, juicy stems and foliage of these plants are normally killed by frost, and the plants overwinter underground as roots, rhizomes, bulbs, tubers, or corms, sending up new growth each spring.

In the warmer areas, zones 8 to 10, perennials may be deciduous or they may turn woody, depending on the severity of the winter and the type of plant. If the above-ground parts of perennials try to persist over the winter, warm-zone gardeners can pretend they are Jack Frost and mow them off at ground level with a lawn mower around the first of the year.

Perennials tend to have relatively short seasons of bloom—two or three weeks a season, typically, although some, like coreopsis, will bloom all season once they get started, and some will flower in spring, relax over the summer, then give a repeat bloom in mild-weather autumns.

A stroll through the perennial garden can be as appealing to the nose as to the other senses; some perennials produce sensuous and even sensual fragrances, like the tropical smell of the August lily (*Hosta plantaginea*). Because perennials are usually planted in small groups, however, they do not ordinarily perfume the air like huge masses of flowering shrubs and trees do. A mature mock orange (*Philadelphus coronaria*) will make a mound twenty feet (6.1 meters) in diameter and fifteen feet (4.6 meters) high, covered entirely with richly fragrant white blossoms, and can thus fill the yard with scent. But it would take a huge bed of strongly fragrant perennials to do the same thing. We should not expect our perennials to perfume the whole property. While some can scent the air, most have fragrances that are more discrete, for the nose that approaches with intent to discern whether the flower carries a smell.

The following perennials are those commonly sold varieties most noted for their fragrance. The list is by no means exhaustive, however, as there are literally thousands of fragrant perennials.

Bee balm (*Monarda fistulosa*) grows on single stems three feet tall (91.4 cm) with lancelike leaves. The flowers are elaborate little crowns of lavender, with a honey-spice-herb scent all their own. On a sunny day the fragrance hangs in the air like a cloud of scent, attracting bees. Its related garden species, *Monarda didyma,* comes in red, pink, and white, but does not have the flower fragrance of *M. fistulosa.* It does, however, have the same herbal scent to its leaves.

While most clematis species and varieties are not fragrant, two are noted for their scent. Blue tube clematis (*Clematis heracleifolia* var. *davidiana*) sets out clusters of fragrant, rich blue flowers on a three-foot (91.4 cm) stemmy plant in August and September. In June and July, ground clematis (*C. recta* 'Mandshurica') has fragrant white flowers that project their sweet scent.

Lily of the valley (*Convallaria majalis*) is an old-time favorite that will colonize a choice and shady spot with its low-growing leaves. In spring it produces short racemes with white, bell-like flowers that bear a clean, soft floral scent much beloved by everyone who smells it.

Crinum is a tender bulbous perennial with bright green, straplike leaves and large, pink to white, trumpet-shaped flowers in late spring or early summer. The bulbs should be planted in pots in cold-winter areas and brought indoors when freezing nights arrive. The flowers have a simple, direct, sweet, and light floral scent.

One of the most interesting flower scents is the distinctive chocolate scent of *Cosmos atrosanguineus,* which emanates from chocolate-colored flowers borne in late summer on airy, two- to three-foot (61 to 91.4 cm) plants. My chocolate cosmos is mixed with the silver-leaved dusty miller (*Senecio cineraria*) for a striking visual and olfactory effect.

Almost all the different species and cultivars of dianthus—carnations, cheddar pinks, maiden pinks, and cottage pinks—have a rich, spicy scent of cloves. The leaves tend to be gray-green to blue-green, making them easy to work into the medium green perennials. But place your

---

OPPOSITE. *The leaves of bee balm (*Monarda didyma*), just opening a few red flowers at the bottom of these massive stone steps at Old Westbury Gardens, Old Westbury, New York, give off a strong herbal scent when crushed between the fingers. The fingers can then be wiped against the soft seed heads of* Pennisetum alopecuroides.

ABOVE: *The perfume of peonies, such as this white peony (*Paeonia lactiflora*) photographed in France, is a constant delight to gardeners in cold areas.*

OPPOSITE TOP: *Tree peonies (*Paeonia suffruticosa*), like these growing with Spanish bluebells (*Endymion hispanicus*) at the Princess Sturdza garden in La Vasterival in Varengeville-sur-mer, France, are as beautiful as herbaceous peonies (*Paeonia lactiflora*), but not as fragrant.*

OPPOSITE BOTTOM: *The sweet smell of wallflowers (*Cheiranthus*) wafts upwards from a bed of iris swords in the Geri Laufer Garden in Atlanta, Georgia. You may notice the scent of a thick stand of wallflowers from several feet away.*

dianthus where visitors can get at them, for their scent is noticeable only when your nose is right upon the flowers.

Sweet woodruff (*Asperula* or *Galium odoratum*) is a groundcover for shady spots and produces small clusters of tiny white flowers in spring. These are used to flavor May wine in Germany, and make a perfect nosegay when tied into a bunch. The scent is a light vanilla-herb-haylike fragrance that keeps you coming back for another whiff.

Common heliotrope (*Heliotropium arborescens*) has purplish-green leaves and violet to white flower clusters on stemmy plants. The flowers' delicate, sweet fragrance is similar to, but stronger than, that of dame's rocket (*Hesperis matronalis*) or money plant (*Lunaria biennis*).

Most hostas are grown for their elegant, expansive foliage, but August lily, also known as fragrant plantain lily (*Hosta plantaginea*), is rather unremarkable of form. When August arrives, however, it shows its true talent by sending up a two-foot spike with white, trumpet-shaped flowers heavily scented with a tropical fragrance, almost like tuberose. This fragrance carries on the air, especially at night.

Hyacinths of many species grow in spring from bulbs, but it seems that every market in America sells massed pots of *Hyacinthus orientalis* around Easter time, and the scent can be almost overpowering in such profusion. A few hyacinths in the garden, however, can put a subtle sweet scent on the air. Grape hyacinths (*Muscari botryoides*) are not related to ordinary hyacinths, but they are also nicely fragrant with a sweet floral scent.

Sweet pea (*Lathyrus odoratus*) is a late spring and summer annual worth mentioning because of its clean, sweet scent. Grown in profusion, sweet peas are exuberant in shades of rose, lavender, cream, white, blue, amethyst, purple, and scarlet.

The most fragrant lilies are selected species, rather than the big, hybrid garden types. Probably the most pleasantly scented is the white Madonna lily (*Lilium candidum*), followed by goldband lily (*L. auratum*). The florists' fragrant Easter lily is *Lilium longiflorum*, a type that normally blooms in summer but is forced for the Easter holiday. If you set this in the garden after it blooms in the spring, it may bloom again in the autumn, and then in midsummer in subsequent years. Florists' lilies may transmit viruses, so keep them apart from other lilies.

Wallflowers (*Cheiranthus cheiri*) are bushy plants that develop their flowering stem tops at about the same time as tulips and lilacs, with which they associate beautifully. The flowers come in velvety yellow, orange, purple, red, and rose, depending on the cultivar, and have a distinctive fragrance of floral perfumes. I first encountered this scent on a California bluff overlooking the Pacific Ocean. Soft, brownish yellow flowers bloomed atop stems kept short by the relentless west wind. I had to get down on all fours to reach them with my nose, and was there greeted with the most divine scent. The cultivated species are not quite as fragrant, but worthwhile nevertheless.

One of the chief joys of the cold-area gardener is the peony, especially the Chinese peony (*Paeonia lactiflora*), whose golf-ball–size buds open to huge, double flowers up to ten inches (25.4 cm) across, perfumed with the scent of roses. (Tree peonies and other species lack this kind of fragrance.) These perennials have pretty leaves much used in Chinese paintings. The big blooms are short-lived, unfortunately, and a rain during their short bloom will bend them down and turn them to brown mush.

Stock (*Matthiola incana*) is a pretty biennial or perennial usually grown as a late-summer annual. It reaches two to three feet (61 to 91.4 cm) in height, has narrow leaves, and produces its flower clusters at

the stem tips. The flower colors are yellow, cream, white, pink, red, lavender, and blue, and it is best grown in masses. Its chief feature, however, is the billows of floral fragrance it gives off.

Among the daffodils, the jonquils (*Narcissus jonquilla* hybrids) are the fragrant beauties. They bloom after the regular daffodils, and their perfume is quite rich and heavy, although it does not carry.

One perennial usually grown as a summer annual is *Nicotiana;* there are two very fragrant species. The most fragrant is *N. sylvestris,* which grows to five feet (1.5 meters) and carries long, tubular white flowers in tiers. It has an intense, sweet floral scent. Less strong but still aromatic is *N. alata.* These species are much more fragrant than the hybrid strains often sold in seed packets.

German, or bearded, irises produce soft and subtle sweet scents that vary according to flower color. It is always a treat to try to guess what a new cultivar will smell like from the color of its petals.

Perhaps the most intense scent of any perennial is given by tuberose (*Polianthes tuberosa*). This tropical species can be planted in pots or set into the garden or border and will bloom annually in late summer. The tubers must be taken up, like dahlias and begonias, after bloom is finished, and stored away from freezing temperatures. Tuberose smells like a tropical forest—heady, intense, rich, and spicy-floral. A few pots on the porch will afford a treat for anyone who sits outdoors on a warm summer night.

Moonlight primrose is the romantic common name of *Primula alpicola.* In the summer, the clumps of large leaves send up eighteen-inch (45.7 cm) stalks with clusters of yellow, bell-shaped flowers that produce a particularly sharp floral fragrance.

Although it is an annual, not a perennial, mignonette (*Reseda odorata*) must be mentioned. Its short clumps of ungainly plants bear inconspicuous—some would say unattractive—flowers in loose, green and brownish yellow clusters. Fortunately, it has a beautiful scent. Plant a bed below a porch railing on the south side of the house, as this is one herbaceous plant whose gorgeous scent carries far.

Sweet violet (*Viola odorata*) is the small, familiar plant with heart-shaped leaves and early spring flowers sweetly and lightly scented when smelled at very close range. It tends to take over favored spots, but few gardeners object, because it makes a good-looking ground cover with little effort on the gardener's part.

Many other perennials and annuals have scented flowers, but these common types are available at nurseries and through catalogs, and they would be the mainstays of any fragrance garden.

LEFT. *Bearded iris (*Iris germanica *hybrids) border a path at Monet's Garden in Giverny, France. These flowers provide a smorgasbord for the nose, as the scent of each iris suggests its color: white of vanilla, purple of grape, and so on.*

ABOVE. *Visually, the chief interest of this private Connecticut garden is the stone obelisk and the arresting oaklike leaves of* Hydrangea quercifolia *in the background. But if we were standing there, the lovely hanging trumpets of white-flowered datura (*Brugmansia candida*) to the right of the hydrangea might catch our interest first, as they fill the space with a rich, deep perfume projected over many yards, especially at night.*

SWEET SCENTS IN THE DARKNESS

For some reason, the fragrance of flowers seems more mysterious, romantic, and sensual at night. Perhaps the reason is that when the visual sense is shut down, the senses of smell and touch become more acute. Whatever the cause, gardeners have planted their trysting places with sweet-smelling, night-blooming plants for centuries. In fact, some plants are best known for their night scents. We have already mentioned the August lily (*Hosta plantaginea*) among the perennials, but all types of plants can fill the night with romantic scents. The so-called night-blooming jasmine (*Cestrum nocturnum*) is a familiar example. One can almost set one's watch by the regularity with which it perfumes the air after the sun goes down. It blooms on and off again throughout the year. One specimen I grew in a pot in Pennsylvania faithfully opened its heavily scented blossoms for Christmas.

Lady-of-the-night (*Brunfelsia americana*) also waits for dark to reveal its charms; this cousin of the common plant called yesterday, today, and tomorrow (*Brunfelsia pauciflora*) may be hard to find, however. More commonly available is the datura (*Brugmansia candida*), a rather rank plant that will grow from six to ten feet (1.8 to 3 meters) tall in a season and sets out very large, white, downward-hanging trumpets, in summer and again in fall, that perfume the air around them at night. The white flowers glow in the moonlight, too, making them doubly romantic. They are not hardy outdoors in areas colder than Zone 9. Grown indoors, they are best treated as a small, woody tree.

Wax plant (*Hoya carnosa*) produces clusters of waxy, white flowers that are particularly fragrant in the evening. Its scent is spicy, intense, and sweet.

An annual that perfumes the night is scented evening stock (*Matthiola longipetala bicornis*). During the day, the sun keeps its purple flowers closed, but at night they open to pour their fragrance into the air.

We have been describing pleasantly scented flowers, but of course there are some with unpleasant scents, and a few whose pleasingness is subject to debate. Some scents are arguably "off." Some people, for instance, think the world of *Cestrum nocturnum*, but a friend of mine thinks it smells like hot dogs and is far too intense. Most of the "off" scents in flowers are mildly objectionable, such as the cloying smell of *Amaryllis belladonna*. Some are downright disgusting, like the smell of the succulent *Stapelia*, or starfish flower, often grown as a houseplant.

FRAGRANT BARKS AND ROOTS

Barks and roots have scents, too, but these fragrances do not become evident in the garden unless the plant is uprooted or cut into. In my boyhood, we often cut small branches from black birch (*Betula lenta*) and cut curls of their bark into a pot of boiling water to make rich, reddish brown birch tea with its strong aroma of wintergreen. Today birch oil is commonly distilled from this plant to make birch beer or, mixed with other extracts, root beer.

The hedgerows of the East are usually overrun with sassafras (*Sassafras albidum*), which is a small, woody, weed tree in the North and a larger tree in the South. Its twigs are fragrant when crushed, but it is in the roots where the inimitable scent and flavor of sassafras are concentrated. Digging up a sassafras root was always the very first act of spring back East, and was performed when the soil finally thawed.

One reason digging out a sassafras root for tea is so much fun is that you first become aware of the sweet, wintergreen, teaberry, pine scent by merely digging in the earth around the roots. From the soil of winter, at last freed from the deep winter's ice, comes the scent of spring itself. You grasp a root and pull it up to expose it, then use the shovel to chop it off. The temperature may be in the thirties that day, but with that summer-sweet root in your pocket, you know spring has now begun in earnest. The sap is flowing sweetly in the maples. From the winter-right buds on the roots, corms, and bulbs under the ground, new growth is pushing—even if it has not yet reached the surface.

It took me years to figure out that the sassafras essence is concentrated in the reddish material that sheaths the roots. I used to make my spring tea from chunks of the whole root, but eventually I learned to wash and scrub the root to get rid of its thin, outer bark, revealing a reddish layer of corky material underneath. I slice this off the slippery, woody roots in long, thin strips. These are allowed to air dry. If thoroughly dry, the aromatic sassafras chips will keep for a year. Tales tell of American pioneers using sassafras as a tea when they could not get the store-bought variety. Considering the quality of the aroma, one wonders why the pioneers consumed it in such small quantities—they must have known that in large amounts it can be dangerous. Sassafras contains a compound thought to be a carcinogen; drinking sassafras tea on a regular basis should be avoided. A yearly springtime cup of fresh sassafras tea probably will not hurt, however.

The bearded iris 'Florentina', the least ostentatious of all its tribe, quietly opens its greyish white flowers in May. Its flower has a sweet scent, and its root smells most wonderfully of violets. When the root is dried and powdered, it is known as orrisroot and is used to preserve the scent of dried flowers in potpourris.

Many other roots are scented, but most root fragrances are fairly inconspicuous. Angelica, however, has a nice spicy scent.

LEAF SCENTS AND HERBS

A major part of the overall smell of a garden on a sunny day is the aroma of the volatile oils in leaves. The leaf scents differ from the flowery scents because of their function. Flower fragrances are used by plants to attract pollinators, but the volatile oils in leaves are believed to discourage leaf-eating insects. These oils tend to be pungent, aromatic, medicinal, and intense.

The Mediterranean, or culinary, herbs tend to have such oils in abundance, and we are all familiar with the fragrances of sage, rosemary, thyme, and oregano. Eucalyptus represents the downside of this scent, and huge stands of it in California cover large areas with an unpleasant odor that, when intense, is reminiscent of cat urine. Among the herbs are dill, anise, basil, anise-scented fennel, lavender, celery-scented lovage, and real French tarragon. Sometimes the seeds of herb plants are aromatic, too; anise seed and coriander (the seed of the cilantro plant) are examples.

Not all leaf smells are pungent and volatile, however. Scented geraniums (*Pelargonium* spp.) give off smells as diverse as herbs, flowers, fruits, and spices. Among the most common "flavors" of the leaves are apple-scented (*Pelargonium odoratissimum*), lime-scented (*P. nervosum*), lemon-scented (*P. crispum*), peppermint-scented (*P. tomentosum*), and rose-scented (*P. graveolens*) geraniums.

These geraniums are best used along a path in the garden, or grown in pots where passersby can rub a leaf and enjoy the mimicking of other fragrances by these plants. Citrusy, lemony scents are fairly common in plant leaves. Well-known examples are lemon thyme (*Thymus citriodorus*), lemon verbena (*Aloysia triphylla*), and lemon balm (*Melissa officinalis*).

The familiar smell of mint (*Mentha* spp.) comes from the oil-producing sacs in the leaf axils of this plant. Among the strongest mints are Corsican mint (*Mentha requienii*), a mat-forming creeper with an intense, minty scent, and pennyroyal (*M. pulegium*), with an odor so strong it is repellent.

One of those plants that touches our senses of fragrance and sight at the same time is the creeping, vine-like *Houttuynia cordata* 'Variegata' (also sold as *Houttuynia cordata* 'Chameleon'). Its ivy-shaped leaves are splotched with yellow, red, pink, and cream, and they have a distinct orange-peel scent when crushed. *Houttuynia* is a good plant to pot for a shady porch, where it can be seen and smelled. When first spotted, *Houttuynia* can be striking in appearance; its orange-peel fragrance takes second billing to the sharp variegations of its thick foliage.

The needle pines—the firs, hemlocks, pines, cedars, and arborvitae—are a group of plants with a familiar, fresh, resinous scent. This scent is probably most clearly and cleanly expressed in the balsam fir (*Abies balsamea*), which is native to the northeastern United States. Most pines, when their bark is cut, exude a clear, gel-like resin that smells intensely of pine.

ABOVE: *Fresh, bracing herbal scents fill the garden on sunny mornings when the plantings include the Mediterranean herbs like rosemary, thyme, lavender, oregano, and sage. Here at the Beth Chatto Garden at Elmstead Market, Colchester, England, Spanish lavender (*Lavandula stoechas*) is in full bloom along with the round flower balls of *Allium aflatunense, the green flowers of *Euphorbia wulfenii, and the white *Penstemon 'Evelyn'.

OPPOSITE: *A garden of Mediterranean herbs gives off a heady, clean smell that can be used to repel some insects from treasured plantings. In the foreground, dark green Santolina virens *grows with the gray-white* Santolina chamaecyparissus. *In the background, English lavender (*Lavandula angustifolia*) is blooming, while at right a large bush of rosemary (*Rosmarinus officinalis*) sports tiny blue flowers along its stems. All these herbs give off strong scents when crushed. The garden is that of Bill Slater in Santa Barbara, California.*

BEAUTIFULLY SCENTED HERBS

Some flowers keep their scent when dried; old European roses and hyssop are two good examples. The champion in this regard is pearly everlasting (*Anaphalis triplinervis*, sometimes found as *A. cinnamomea*). This hardy perennial has fine, silver-gray leaves; in late summer it produces masses of oystershell-white, fluffy, long-lasting clusters of small, pearly flowers with small, yellow centers. A wild species, *A. margaritacea*, is found over the entire North American continent, from west coast to east, and from northernmost Alaska to Central America. All these species of *Anaphalis* have a thick, fragrant smell of flowery hay—intriguing, dry, intense. The flowers themselves are everlasting and are choice members of any dried arrangement both for their appearance and their fragrance, present even when dried. For some reason, this scent seems to intensify when mixed in the dried arrangement with the camphorous scents of the gray-leaved plants such as *Santolina*, the artemisias, tansy, and the ornamental yarrows (*Achillea* spp.).

SAVING THE SCENTS
OF SUMMER

It is possible to preserve the fragrance of the summer garden in a potpourri. When potpourri is mentioned, most people think of a basket of dried flowers sitting on the table. These dried potpourri are usually doctored with the essential oils of flowers—rose attar, lemon oil, rosemary oil, and so forth—to keep their aroma. Exposed to air, most dried potpourris last only a few months before losing their scent.

The traditional French way of making potpourri is more romantic, more fun, and reflects the meaning of the French word. Potpourri literally means "rotten pot." A moist mixture of rose petals and other aromatic plant flowers and leaves, plus spices, it is kept not in baskets, but in special potpourri jars.

Old-fashioned potpourri jars have two lids. The perforated inner lid lets the scent out, while a solid outer one keeps the fragrance inside until it is wanted. If you can find one or more of these, by all means pick them up, for they are not easy to find. Pots with single perforated lids are much more abundant. Any small ceramic pot with a tight-fitting lid will do, however. Simply take the top off when the scent is wanted.

The basic ingredient of moist potpourri is rose petals. With most roses, however, the scent is evanescent, while we seek permanence. Thus, certain old-fashioned roses are needed, specifically China roses, Bourbon roses, cabbage and moss

ABOVE: *Flowers often refer to several senses at once. "Rose" not only means the plant and its flowers, such as these 'Friendship' roses in Manito Park in Spokane, Washington, but also a color and a scent.*

OPPOSITE: *The heavenly scents of roses and lavender mingle and emanate from a fence in Ruth Bancroft's garden in Walnut Creek, California.*

ABOVE: *A hint of old-fashioned roses lingers near the pretty blossoms of these peonies (*Paeonia officinalis*) at the Chelsea Physic Garden in London.*

OPPOSITE: *A good strategy for scented plants is to grow some in pots. When they bloom, they can be moved onto a deck or porch where people congregate, then located to a less frequented spot when out of bloom. This group in a private garden designed by Tish Rehill on Long Island, New York, includes the bright gold* Lantana camara *'Allgold', whose leaves when crushed have a pungent smell. A rose begins to bloom nearby and against the wall in the background the surpassingly lovely* Mandevilla *'Alice duPont' blooms freely.*

roses (*Rosa centifolia*), damask roses, French roses (*R. gallica*), and cultivars of *Rosa rugosa*.

Harvest the roses in the morning, between ten and eleven o'clock, selecting only those that are half-opened. Avoid full-blown roses, for much of their scent has already flown on the wind. During the peak bloom, harvest roses every day. Pick off the green calyxes and stems and spread the petals on screens, out of direct sunlight, for one day. They will not dry, but will turn leathery.

Measure two packed cups of petals into the crock, then add one-fourth cup of kosher salt. Layer petals and salt until your day's picking is stored. Cover the surface of the petals with a plate that is slightly smaller than the crock interior, and weight it with a stone or brick, then cover. The salt makes the petals' juice flow. Each day add more petals until the crock is nearly full or until fresh roses are no longer available. Stir before every addition of petals, and replace the plate with the weight and cover on the fresh layer. Keep track of the number of layers.

When you run out of petals, add one-fourth cup (56.7 gms) of powdered orrisroot for every two cups (453.6 gms) of rose petals. Stir thoroughly and allow it to cure until October. This mixture, called the stock, is dull brown, pasty, and smells richly of roses.

During the summer, cut fresh flower spikes of lavender, either English lavender (*Lavandula angustifolia*) or French lavender (*L. dentata*); the English has the better scent. Dry these in a cool, dry place and store them away.

Throughout the growing season, cut into pieces, dry, and store in tight glass jars leaves of the following plants: pineapple sage (*Salvia elegans*), hyssop, calendula, costmary, basil, angelica, California bay (in the West) or bayberry (in the East), lemon or caraway thyme, bee balm (*Monarda didyma* or *M. fistulosa*), lemon balm, sassafras, and scented geraniums (*Pelargonium*).

Potpourri mixing time arrives in October. Begin the process by preparing a blend of equal amounts of whole spices, such as cardamom, cloves, cinnamon, nutmeg, mace, vanilla bean, caraway, coriander, anise seed, dried wintergreen berries, dried ginger, and black peppercorns. Go easy on the ginger and peppercorns. Also dry citrus peel in thin strips and add it to the mixture. Now crush the whole fairly finely in a mortar and pestle.

For each quart (1 liter) of stock, add one level tablespoon of the crushed spice mixture. Add two cups (453.6 gms) of dried lavender flowers for a rose-lavender aroma. If you want roses to predominate, add less lavender.

Add the dried leaves from the jars to fine-tune the mixture. If it needs a high note, add leaves like salvia, lemon balm, angelica, and costmary. If it needs more bass, add basil, caraway thyme, and bay. Avoid the temptation of using equal amounts of all the leaves. Use them as you would use culinary spices in cooking: to adjust the flavor, or rather the fragrance.

When everything is added, mix thoroughly and allow to cure weighted with a plate and brick as before. Cover for four to six weeks, then spoon into potpourri jars. As you use these jars, stir them occasionally to work up fresh scent. Ones with perforated covers can be placed in drawers.

Unlike dried flowers, moist-method potpourri holds its scent, even intensifying it over time, and stays aromatic for years.

If you like the appearance of dried flowers, again depend on the old-fashioned roses, but choose ones that are pink in bud, as this color is kept when dry (white roses turn brown, red roses turn black). Rose petals and scented leaves of other plants can be dried in a warm oven (no more than 150 degrees) for a short while, until they are thoroughly dry but not brittle. Allow some whole buds to dry as well, and mix the result with the dried leaves, lavender, and orrisroot in the proportions given for moist potpourri. Do not use the spices, however.

Potpourri can be used around the house, but not usually outside on the porches. Training fragrant vines up the porch post works to perfume the air where people sit and relax. Honeysuckle, *Clematis paniculata, Trachelospermum jasminoides, Mandevilla laxa,* climbing fragrant roses, wisteria, and many other fragrant climbers can be used in this way.

You can also grow fragrant plants in pots and containers on the porch. Particularly suited are mignonette, stock, gardenias, wallflowers (*Cheiranthus cheiri*), and scented geraniums (*Pelargonium*). A porch lined with containers of these plants will be filled with a heavenly scent all summer.

Touch

I felt the rain's cool fingertips
Brushed tenderly across my lips.
Edna St. Vincent Millay

As a cat prowls in the dark, her long whiskers reach out on all sides to feel the edges and walls and corridors through which she passes. These stiff hairs help her sense things at a distance from her face, giving her warning, expanding her ability to feel.

Because the hair has no nerves in the shafts, it can be bitten, scratched, cut, and even burned without pain. The hair follicle buried in the skin, on the other hand, is connected to nerve endings so exquisitely sensitive that the merest movement of the hair is felt. So, while it does not hurt a cat to cut its whiskers, it hurts to pull on them.

Similarly, the hair on our bodies gives us our first indication that something is touching us. Hold your forearm in front of you and gently run your fingertips just above the skin. The hair on the arms—fine though it may be—sends signals to the neurons attached to the ends of the hair shafts, and we can feel the passing of the fingertips although nothing has touched the skin. If an insect or a person we do not like touches us like that, it gives us the creeps. But if someone we love does it, such a whisper of a touch is welcome. The touch is the same event physically, but in a different world psychologically. Whether a touch pleases us, displeases us, or is neutral, it is always firmly subject to our understanding of what is happening. The touch that may be pleasurable on one part of the body can be painful on another, because the nerves that sense touch are more densely packed into some areas than others.

Repetition can turn a good touch bad. A few strokes on our skin feel comforting and good. But if the same place is stroked again and again, it may be annoying or even painful. Some touches are positively healing. A mother's hand on the brow of a fevered child, a healer's touch on an ill person, the touch of the earth. This last touch is mysterious and wonderful, and quite powerful.

LEFT. *Wood rounds keep our boots out of the winter mud along this path lined with heath (*Erica*) at the Van Dusen Botanical Garden in Vancouver, British Columbia. At times when we are lost to our human problems, the touch of mud and the grounding earth are a balm for our harried spirits.*

PAGES 112-113. *A very soft, inviting pot of plants includes the little daisies of* Erigeron *'Profusion' and the violet cups of* Nierembergia hippomanica. *The pot is set up within easy reach of curious passersby at Old Westbury Gardens, Old Westbury, New York.*

TACTILE FACETS OF THE GARDEN

Every true gardener knows that one of the chief joys of this activity is working deeply with the soil, pushing one's hands deep into its moist, life-giving crumbliness.

It takes about three years for structureless, caked, hard, dry dirt to turn into rich soil. In one of my first gardens, the ground was like concrete in the spring. I had to use a pick to open rows for vegetables! I added compost to the rows so the vegetables would have some nutrition, and mulched the rows with deep layers of rooted corn silage. That year, nothing much grew except the greenbrier and the burdock, but it was a start. That winter the mulch decayed and loosened the top few inches of soil.

The next spring, I was able to turn the soil with a shovel, which gave me a chance to pick some of the biggest rocks out of it. I contracted with a local farmer to spread six inches (15.2 cm) of cow manure over the whole vegetable garden with his manure spreader, and then to turn the fresh manure into the soil with his plow.

That summer I grew a dense crop of gorgeous, dark green weeds, and along with them, a respectable set of

RIGHT. *Some trees demand that we touch them, if just for the fun of crumbling off a bit of exfoliating bark with our fingertips. This river birch (*Betula nigra*) is growing in the garden of Princess Sturdza in La Vasterival in Varengeville-sur-mer, France.*

ABOVE. *The rose has a coarse texture, as contrasted with the fine-textured plant at its feet. This pair of opposites is charming on an old stone railing at Wallington garden in Cambo, England.*

OPPOSITE TOP. *Some flowers invite touch, such as these just-opening flower plumes of* Filipendula ulmaria. *They are greenish now but will turn into creamy white clouds of florets as they open. Below them grow the choice veined leaves and flowers of fringe cups (*Tellima grandiflora*). Geranium* psilostemon *and* Meconopsis *add sparks of color to this bed at the Joseph Woods Garden in Avon, England.*

OPPOSITE BOTTOM. *A stone path winds through drifts of lamb's ears (*Stachys byzantina*), perhaps the most inviting of all garden leaves to touch. Lamb's ears and small clumps of candytuft (*Iberis sempervirens*) are used to brighten the path through the Jim and Connie Cross Garden in Cutchogue, New York.*

vegetables. There was enough nutrition in that soil to grow beanstalks the size of grapevines. Again I cultivated the weeds by chopping them into the soil with a hoe and then mulching the whole area with thick pads of spoiled hay. Over the winter the hay decayed, this time mixing with the decayed manure to turn the top six inches (15.2 cm) of soil rich, dark, moist, and crumbly.

The third spring, I had a ton of mushroom compost hauled in and spread it thickly over all the vegetable beds, then turned it in two shovels deep. It took work, but from then on, decaying mulch was all I needed to keep the soil so rich and fluffy that I used to impress my friends by plunging my arms up to the elbows into the garden soil.

I recount this soil-building story because this process works, even on bad soils. Well-worked, heavily improved soil gives you a healthy garden, whether vegetable or ornamental. Making compost and improving soil gives you the chance to get your hands into the ground and feel the immense calmness and centeredness of the earth, and to touch the matrix from which we came and to which we will eventually return. Good soil has a crumbly, moist feel that is pleasant to the touch.

The sense of touch is not usually the most forward sense, but it can be given more prominence in certain passages of the landscape if we provide for it. Being bluntly obvious with tactile experience in the garden may be the best way to bring it to full consciousness, as it ordinarily sings in the chorus of our senses, rather than taking a solo. Place

plants, stones, or sculptures where people cannot miss touching them. Otherwise, as they daydream down your paths, they might pass by without stopping to feel a gritty wall, a pearled shell set in concrete, a bank of moss, or the petals of a full-blown peony blossom that falls apart in the hand.

Too many gardens are built simply to present a pretty picture. A garden is a picture people can move through. How much more enjoyable is the garden experience when the visitor is always being surprised by the way the garden anticipates and fulfills the subconscious desires of the senses! Such gardens reveal their makers—not with words, but with deeds: the fragrant roses that tumble nose-high above the path; a stone for rubbing beside the garden bench; a pool of springwater with a soft mat of moss for kneeling provided at just the right spot to take a drink.

Greenery can soothe us with its touch. Imagine lying down in the middle of a meadow of tall grasses, face up, with the sunny sky a million miles wide above, and the earth reduced to the soft nest of grass that rises up all around us.

Grasses are one of the most tactile of garden plants. They belong on the edge of a garden path, hanging into the path so that we have to brush their slender leaves and soft seed heads aside as we pass through.

Plants with real tactile appeal include the feathery leaves of mimosa (*Albizia julibrissin*), which can be planted about ten to fifteen feet (3 to 4.5 meters) back from the path so that its branch tips hang the leaves within reach of visitors. In flower, the mimosa's white and pinkish red puffy flowers are like lights on the tree and are effective in nighttime illumination.

The hard shadows cast by night illumination tend to accentuate the tactile aspects of plants. I once saw a devil's-walking-stick (*Aralia spinosa*) under nighttime illumination. This spiny plant is fearsome enough in the daytime, and at night its wicked thorns were positively spooky.

Plants can heal us, too. While I was out fishing one day, a bee stung me on the little finger, evidently injecting its venom into a vein that went straight back to my heart, for within a few minutes, my body was covered with a hot, itchy rash, and my head pounded with intense pressure. When I got home, my friend gathered the leaves of rib-eye plantain, crushed them, and rubbed my body down with them. The itching stopped immediately. The next morning, the only rash on my body was from the ankles down—the only parts she did not rub with plantain juice.

Touching plants can also harm us. Oleander, for instance, is extremely poisonous, and its toxins can be absorbed through the skin; poison ivy and poison oak bedevil people across the land; blackberry thorns can tear bloody gashes down our arms when we try to pick a handful of sweet berries.

PLANNING AND PLANTING A TOUCHABLE GARDEN

Despite these caveats, the garden is full of extraordinary things to touch. We too often neglect this sense in the garden in favor of the visual and olfactory senses. By touching, we can add to our sensory impressions of the garden and all that is in it.

Some plants just beg to be touched. If common mullein (*Verbascum thapsus*) did not grow in such wild profusion throughout North America, and were imported from some exotic mountain range in China, there would be no telling what we would pay for its big, silvery-velvet, gray-green leaves, which are as soft as flannel. If mullein volunteers in your garden, by all means care for it. It is a biennial that makes a big basal rosette of leaves the first years and in the second sends up its beautiful velvety flower stalk that opens soft, pale-yellow flowers a few at a time all through the summer.

Another species, called moth mullein (*Verbascum blattaria*), is commonly grown in gardens; there are other ornamental *Verbascums* offered for sale, although none with the degree of silvery velvet found in *V. thapsus*. Other plants are equally appealing to touch. Think of the soft needles of a Lawson cypress, the strange silica feel of horsetail, the feathery leaves of *Dicentra*, the tender and soft leaves of *Mertensia*, the artemisias with their soft, gray-green to silver leaves. (Especially inviting is *Artemisia schmidtiana* 'Silver Mound', which has a soft,

feathery mound of silver silk that you just have to run your hand over.)

Some plants surprise you when you touch them. These include the shrinking leaflets of the sensitive plant or the wild sensitive briar.

Soft and silky plants call out to be touched: silver-gray lamb's ears (*Stachys byzantia*), the amazingly fine-haired leaves of peppermint geranium (*Pelargonium tomentosum*). So do leathery leaves, like those of magnolia, and the shiny, leathery-brown, and green-mottled leaves of trout lilies (*Erythronium americanum*). Some plants invite you not just to touch them, but to lie down on them—ferns, soft mosses, and beds of club moss invite the wanderer to sit, recline, close the eyes for a moment, and be refreshed. Mosses, especially, invite us to stroke them as we rest. Medium-long grasses also invite the passerby to recline. Other grasses—the brushy foxtails of *Pennisetum* and the soft plumes of *Miscanthus sinensis* 'Gracillimus' among them—provide other tactile pleasures.

Some flowers also appeal to our sense of touch. I love to feel the silky, waxy petals of *Magnolia grandiflora;* the foamy white flower heads of the elderberry (*Sambucus canadensis*) are fun to run the palm over, and rose petals remain as delightful to feel as when we were children. Such preferences are to a large extent personal. My daughter-in-law loves to touch the velvety petals of the black pansies (*Viola* spp.), calling them "softer than a butterfly." The smooth, gray bark of American beech (*Fagus grandifolia*) asks to be stroked. The first instinct when coming across the

lacquered smoothness of fresh, red-brown cherry bark flecked with rough lenticels is to touch it, feeling the contrast between the slippery bark and the speed bumps. The same instinct engages when seeing the similarly polished silvery bark of yellow birch (*Betula alleghaniensis*).

At the other end of the scale, the stinging nettle (*Urtica dioica*) volunteers in gardens, shady meadows, and woodland edges everywhere east of the Great Basin. Its leaves bristle with tubules filled with formic acid—the same substance contained in an ant's sting, and a potent chemical compound. One touch and the skin stings, and continues to sting, for several hours. Even the lightest touch of stinging nettles can be quite painful. Fortunately, the old rule that poisons in nature are usually accompanied by their antidotes holds true here. Common burdock (*Arctium minus*) usually grows near stinging nettles, whose sting can be ameliorated by burdock juice squeezed from its stems.

Another example of this rule is the effect of the juice of jewelweed (*Impatiens biflora*) on poison ivy blisters. If you catch the rash early and apply jewelweed juice regularly,

---

OPPOSITE. *All sorts of surfaces call for our touch in this scene at the Royal Botanic Garden of Edinburgh in Scotland: the water to touch with our fingertips, the cold mud beneath its surface to feel on our hands, the stones for our feet, the upstanding golden and green swords of* Iris pseudacorus *'Variegata' to bounce our palms on, and the soft, plump leaves of* Hosta sieboldiana *to sweep our hands over when we cross the stepping stones.*

the rash will begin disappearing in a couple of days, rather than in the week or so usually required. In addition to the toxic plants, there are those plants that rebuff our touch—the cacti, spiny *Euphorbia*s, spiky-edged hollies, and many others. For sheer pain, as long as we are on the subject, few plants beat the barbs of the Teddy Bear cholla (*Opuntia bigelovii*). Despite its name, this decidedly uncuddly plant produces a deep, striking pain accompanied by a burning ache when one of its wicked spikes penetrates the skin.

There is a perversity in human nature that prompts us to test a plant's sharp thorns and spines with a touch of our thumb. Pointed bumps on leaves, as along the *Aloe vera* and several other succulents, or the husks of the horse chestnut seed, give us a goosey feeling when stroked. The hard, uninviting shells of seeds and nuts are frequently felt, not for pleasure, but as a way to get to the food within. There is a satisfying feeling in prying apart the thick, corky shell segments of the hickory (*Carya ovata*).

The shagbark hickory tree, by the way, has all kinds of wonderful parts to touch, starting with the great, shaggy, exfoliating bark sections, the crumbly catkins that hang from the base of the unfolding leaves in the spring, the smooth nut itself inside the shell, and the shiny, oily, brown meat inside. When you penetrate to the meat of the nut, the tree becomes a multisensory experience, for nothing tastes like a hickory nut: rich, intense, packed with nutty flavors, and pervasive when added to other ingredients, as in a hickory

nut torte (heaven on earth).

It is fun to strip off the papery husks of filberts, both wild (*Corylus americana*) and domesticated (*Corylus* hybrids). The pebbly, green husks of black walnuts (*Juglans nigra*) are interesting when rubbed briefly like a baseball between the palms, at least until they start to turn soft. These husks quickly decay into a black ooze that puts a next-to-permanent stain on the hands. Allowed to dry out, they can be removed from the rough, pitted nuts if you use gloves. After curing, the nuts produce a meat nearly as intense as the hickory's, but distinct in flavor—less sweet and rich than a hickory's, with a slightly resinous bitterness.

When I was a child in the first and second grades, the most prized possession of any child in my group was a shiny, reddish brown seed from the horse chestnut (*Aesculus hippocastanum*). These trees seem to have been planted in abundance wherever children walked to and from school, and on the edges of school yards. Although in my adult life I revere them for their beautiful, upstanding, pyramidal flower spikes that decorate the tree in spring, as a child I only noticed them when they dropped their spiny, husked fruits to the pavement. We would pry them apart to collect the prized nuts inside. Part of their appeal, I believe, was the contrast between the forbidding looking spiked husks and the smooth, shiny seeds.

You can increase the tactile interest of your home and garden by hanging and planting interesting things to touch within easy reach:

plants and materials silky and velvety, bristly, pebbly and grainy, and glossy and smooth. A corner of the porch can be decorated with asparagus ferns (*Asparagus densiflorus* 'Sprengeri') offering their fronds for fondling from overhead pots, the complicated blossoms of passionflowers (*Passiflora alatocaerulea*) blooming along the porch rail and waiting for a scientific mind to pull them apart, a planter set with stones, placed in a sea of woolly thyme (*Thymus lanuginosis*), and an airy puff of baby's breath (*Gypsophila paniculata*) by the steps to wave a hand through as we ascend.

Bamboo invites a touch, with the thumb set into the depression on the side of the cane. Plumey plants always enjoy a good fluffing: *Astilbe, Aruncus, Eremurus, Cimicifuga,* pampas grass—the list is long, and all call to the fingers. But what about the toes?

TOP. *Pebbles set into the cement paving of a garden walkway offer visitors some variation in the feel of the footing even through shoes, but much more so when the bare feet can caress the smooth pebbles and feel the roughness of the cement between them. Aloes, sedums, and pelargoniums cluster in pots beside the white bench in the Beth Chatto Gardens at Elmstead Market, Colchester, England.*

RIGHT. *The visual texture of the cedar (*Cedrus deodara *'White Imp') is soft and silky, but the actual physical texture of the needles is rather hard and prickly to the touch. The cedar grows above a bed of stonecress (*Aethionema grandiflorum*) at the Atlantic Botanic Garden in Atlanta, Georgia.*

BAREFOOT IN THE GARDEN

We touch with our feet as well as our hands, and so the gardener may decide to provide for that aspect of our senses as well. Paths give us a good opportunity to vary materials as the length is traversed, creating a sensual treat that may remain beneath the threshold of full consciousness, but is nevertheless appreciated by visitors as a subtextual part of the garden experience. Path materials should have their forms fit their functions. As functions vary, so will the materials naturally and intelligently. For example, in a low part of the yard, or a wet pond in the terrain, the path may be a boardwalk over the mud. In other places where the sun calls forth too many weeds, the walk can be plain cement or cement set with millions of small, black cabochons, or concretes made with dry paint color added to the wet cement. A shady place may be best served by a path made of soft and spongy shredded barks and natural materials. Big, flat stones can be set craftily to guide visitors up a slope. Bright crunchy gravel may accent a border. Mown grass may be the best material where the path attends a lawn. Even plain bare earth may have its place. All these materials feel different under the feet.

This fact brings to mind the possibility of a "barefoot garden," where friends are invited to take off their shoes and socks as they walk the path through the garden. Their eyes will be drawn to the gardens you have created pathside, but their feet will be occupied adjusting to new and sensuous materials to walk on.

At the natural stopping places along the path, you can place stones or benches for sitting. I once found a stone that formed a natural seat, with perfectly shaped depressions for a human bottom, set at just the right height above the ground. I would walk a mile (1.609 km) or more through the woods to reach that seat. I used to sit there, comfortable in the feeling that the natural world is home and that I was at home in it.

Because of that experience and many others, I am always looking for unusually beautiful stones to bring home to use in the landscaping. They look nice, they function as steps or earth holders in the form of terraces and berms, they can pave the ground or make a wall, and they are tactile, with all kinds of surfaces to touch—from slick, water-worn quartz, to fine-grained slate, to sandy conglomerate, to the roughest granite.

Stones with the most interesting surfaces can be placed beside sitting stones or benches, so that the hand can naturally fall to them and feel them.

Garden structures such as pergolas, benches, and railings can be purchased in extremes of design. Some are stark, industrial, slick enameled metals and burnished aluminum that contrast with the vegetation. Others are very rustic designs recalling the "naturalistic" look of Victorian gardens-in-the-woods. These tend to disappear in the landscape. In either case, the surfaces of these structures are usually very

inviting to the touch. Garden sculptures can be fun to touch if they are made with that purpose in mind. Surfaces such as the burnished copper or brass used as liquid shapes in a modern design are so inviting to touch that they are sometimes incorporated into fountains where water can continuously lave them.

ABOVE. *If we cannot reach the bark to touch it with our hands, we can at least get a vicarious experience as other plants touch it. Here in Princess Sturdza's garden, we see an ivy (*Hedera helix*) feeling its way up the trunk of a white birch (*Betula pendula*).*

PAGES 124-125. *This garden is full of things to feel, smell, and see. The grass pathway invites bare feet to walk it. The lamb's ears and light blue flowers of perennial flax (*Linum perenne*), farther along on the right of the path, beg to be touched. In the background, the clipped hedge wants to have its smooth but scratchy surface rubbed by the palm of a hand. The scene is at the garden of the Marquess and Marchioness of Salisbury at Hatfield House, Hatfield, England.*

"TOUCHING" WITH YOUR EYES

Actual texture is quite different from visual texture, that is, the look of a surface and its feel may differ markedly. A surface may look smooth and shiny, but when we go to rub it, it may be sticky, like cellophane tape. A surface may appear rough and pebbly, but feel soft and spongy when we push on it, like some mosses or a sponge. Both visual and tactile senses relate to our sense of a garden's "feeling." For this reason, we will consider visual texture here, along with *real* texture.

In the garden, visual texture is one of the elements we take into account when planning and choosing plants. Mistakes in texture combinations are usually obvious and unattractive. For instance, too many plants with busy, shiny, little evergreen leaves massed together produces a visual sizzle that is quickly tiring to the eyes.

Too much of any type of leaf massed together is unattractive. Contrast is the key to using texture in pleasing and interesting ways. Landscapers talk about visual texture as being fine, medium, and coarse. Fine texture is found in small or very regular leaves, such as the regular tufts of cedar of Lebanon (*Cedrus libani*), or the fine grasses like *Helictotrichon*. Medium visual texture is given by a multitude of plants; *Spiraea* and dogwood are typical examples. Coarse-textured plants usually have large leaves or patterns of leaves that toss this way

and that in irregular motions. *Mahonia bealei* is said to be a coarse-textured plant, as is *Magnolia grandiflora*. Shiny leaf surfaces can add to the impression of coarseness, which is the chief reason, aided by their spiky margins, why hollies look more coarse than medium. Camelias have very shiny leaves, but are usually grown in shade where the glinting sunlight is less strong. Their smooth margins and well-behaved posture give them a medium texture. Variegation can make foliage look busy, but usually does not change its textural impression very much.

Plants with dull or matte leaves give more of a medium impression texturally than shiny ones. Hairy leaves—the woolly *tomentosums* and silver-leaved plants especially—give one an impression of softness that tends to make them look fine. On the other hand, bristly and thorny plants like *Aralia* and rose bushes are considered to be medium to coarse. Saw palmettos and *Washingtonias* are the definition of coarse-textured plants: big, spiky, and tossing this way and that irregularly.

It is not hard to define fine, medium, and coarse visual textures. If a plant looks fine to you, it is fine; if it looks coarse to you, then it is coarse. For the best results in the garden, use a coarse-textured plant with several fine- to medium-textured plants. The coarser the texture of the plant, the more it should be used as an accent in the landscape.

Fine-textured ground covers like bishop's hat (*Epimedium rubrum*) or sweet woodruff (*Asperula* or *Galium odorata*) are generally more pleasing when used across broad areas than

are coarse ones like *Hypericum*. Again, however, contrast is the key. Medium ground covers include plants like pachysandra, periwinkle (*Vinca minor*), and wild ginger (*Asarum europaeum*). One would expect large-leaved ground covers like hostas to give a coarse impression, but their elegant form and often crinkled or seersuckered leaf patterns actually make most of their fine-textured. Only *Hosta plantaginea* creates what I would consider a coarse-leaved impression.

Ferns, even the tall ones, can be used as ground covers and have a variety of textures, although most are soft and fine. Ferns have a stately quality about them—some kind of silence that comes with them from the depths of time, when they were first created. The combination of ferns and hostas is classic, but so is water ringed with a bank of ferns alone under taller shade trees. The airy maidenhair (*Adiantum pedatum*), hay-scented fern (*Dennstaedtia punctilobula*), and lady fern (*Athyrium filix-femina*) all give a fine-textured appearance. Strangely, the beautiful relative of the lady fern called Japanese painted fern (*A. goeringianum*), although in form much like its relative, gives a coarser impression because of areas of variegation coupled with its habit of tossing its leaves about on the ground. Big, vaselike ferns such as cinnamon fern (*Osmunda cinnamomea*) are noble of form but coarse and rough in visual appearance.

Using texture well means varying the surfaces that we see so that they are interesting, folding fine textures into passages of coarse ones,

planting big leaves next to small, shiny next to dull, purple next to lime green, and regular next to wildly irregular.

Sometimes it is fun to throw out all the rules and simply play with texture. In the Golden Gate Park in San Francisco is the Strybing Arboretum—acres and acres of beautiful gardens and fascinating plants. Near a pond is a stand of *Gunnera manicata,* with hairy, bristly leaves from five to eight feet (1.5 to 2.4 meters) across and bristly stems holding the leaves high overhead.

The huge roots hump and plunge into and out of the ground. Sticky looking ferns and thorny plants grow along the edges of the wet, muddy path. It is a scene from a world before time, entirely spiky and bristly, wet and muddy, and it is dramatic, exhilarating, fun, and in a strange way, beautiful.

The sense of touch reveals to us an object's texture. It is the variation of unique and discrete textures that makes something fun to touch and please us, in a way that is more athletic than aesthetic.

ABOVE. *Rough stones dressed and fitted into well-built walls give substance and surfaces solid to touch in an otherwise evanescent garden created for a season out of flowers and foliage. This wonderful mix of stone and plants, with lilacs in bloom along the wall and comfrey (*Symphytum officinale) *at lower right, is found in the garden of Frank and Marjorie Lawley at Herterton House, England.*

Sound

Nine bean rows will I have there,
And a hive for the honey bee,
And live alone in the bee-loud glade.
W. B. Yeats

PAGES 128-129 AND ABOVE. *Clouds, fog, and snow throw a sound-deadening blanket over the world in winter, as at this gazebo at Wayside Gardens in Creston, Canada. On the preceding pages, the same gazebo is seen in summer, where the clear air reveals a vast landscape. Out of the miles of clear air comes something quite the opposite of the muffled sounds of winter: the huge, open, faintly discernible background hum of the world at work.*

I had unearthed a big rock in the middle of the garden and decided to make it the center of my temple—a rough, wooden pergola designed to hold four vines, one at each corner. At the southwest corner was a climbing Don Juan rose; at the northwest, a *Clematis paniculata;* at the northeast corner a wisteria; and at the southeast corner an 'Einset' seedless grape.

The big rock was set into a square of ground I had leveled and paved with flat stones and crushed rock. One day, hot and sweaty from working in the garden, I sat on the rock and for the first time really heard a mockingbird perform.

I realized with intense delight that the bird was indeed mimicking the calls of the other birds, one after the other, rapid-fire, and accurately enough for me to identify several of the birds being imitated. The robin's call, being so familiar, was the one I found myself listening for, and when the mockingbird did its robin, I actually stood up and applauded.

Just as visions of the wilderness show us nature's visual artistry, and the scents of wildflowers show us nature as master perfumer, so do the sounds of nature show us her work as a composer: usually serene and soothing, sometimes hard and strident, but always full of a power so great that we can only wonder at its majesty and mystery.

A stand of pines not far from the house will catch the wailing winter winds and make a rushing, whooshing sound. A strong enough wind will make even the bare trees whistle and the power lines sing. These are dramatic sounds, not ones that calm us.

I believe that it is a sign of the innate goodness of the world that most birdsong is musical. Birds bring their sweet notes from everywhere—a bit of a warble from Brazil, a lonely looping note from the vastness of the far North, a fragment of sweetness stolen from a garden in Central America and brought here to perfume my garden's air with music. This is music we too seldom listen to.

Birdsong is with us almost constantly during the spring and summer daylight hours, and sometimes even at night when a night bird disturbs the world's rest with its mournful call. But it takes an effort on our part to focus on the birds and really listen to them the way we listen to a symphony. Perhaps it is easier to hone in on birdsong when it is not so ubiquitous, as during the winter. In the northeastern United States, the sound of the chickadee ("chickadee-dee-dee") is the melody of a frosty winter day, with the wind blowing bass notes from the trees, and diamond ice tinkling in their branches.

Some years after my mockingbird epiphany, I was privileged to hear John Cage talk about this ability to focus one's attention on the sense of hearing so as to hear and appreciate what is really there. Cage's philosophy held that once the attention is centered on the sense of hearing, the next step is to hear all sound as music: the airplane overhead, the car passing by, the honking horn, the hum of a motor, the sound of an insect, bird, or barking dog—all of it pulsing with natural rhythm, coalescing into a symphony of sound that never ends, but that we can dip into for pleasure whenever we feel like it. There is randomness to it, but also purposefulness, as with a car horn blown several times at intervals, or a bird's song. And, Cage pointed out, through randomness we discover one of the world's operating principles.

RIGHT. *Flowers can suggest music and music can suggest flowers, so closely are they related in our sensibilities. In this corner of Heronswood, a garden designed by Dan Hinkley on Bainbridge Island in Washington, lilies (*Lilium formosanum)* trumpet the high notes and a thick stand of deep violet salvia (*Salvia amplexicaulis)* sounds the bass notes.*

ABOVE. *Ryan Gainey of Decatur, Georgia, has added whimsy to his garden with these charming birdhouses set at different heights. More importantly, he has added bird song, the liquid music that falls softly through the garden and gives life to its aural dimension.*

OPPOSITE. *Birds need cover and food to thrive, and that is provided by a garden with many kinds of plants. This late summer border in a private Connecticut garden offers birds plenty of cover in the conical* Chamaecyparis obtusa *at the left, or the bright fountain of grass (*Miscanthus sinensis 'Variegatus'*) to the right of it. Rose hips dangle in the background, and birds will find seed among the plantings, which include verbena,* Aster frikarti *and* Aster mowa, *artemisia, and* Brassica oleracea.

BIRDSONG IN YOUR GARDEN

To make the most of your garden's auditory gifts, take consciousness there with you on a summer's day. Songbirds vary from place to place, but everyone wants to have these birds as garden visitors:

Bluebirds	Peewees
Bobolinks	Redpolls
Bobwhites	Song sparrows
Buntings	Tanagers
Cardinals	Thrushes
Chickadees	Titmice
Doves	Towhees
Grosbeaks	Veeries
Meadowlarks	Warblers
Mockingbirds	Waxwings
Nuthatches	Whippoorwills
Orioles	Woodpeckers
Phoebes	

We even love the scolding wrens. And best of all, the squawks of pheasant in nearby fields.

Gardeners can attract these and other birds by offering them food and cover. A combination of both is sure to bring birds to the garden. In the cold months you will have to rely on bird feeders to provide food, but in other seasons you can let flora and fauna interact naturally. Try attracting birds with berry-producing plants like viburnums, pyracanthas, dogwoods, Russian olive, and many other berry bushes. Massing these in out-of-the-way corners of the garden—especially the Russian olive (*Elaeagnus angustifolia*), whose berries are most beloved by birds—provides thickets of cover for birds to nest and roost in. By all means, bell your cats, for it is unfair to lure birds to your garden, only to be devoured.

While birds usually dominate the natural soundscape, certain places at certain times can be totally silent. The quieter it is, the vaster the sound of silence becomes, until when it is quiet enough to hear your blood pulsing through your veins, the silence seems infinite. We experience this kind of silence rarely—it can be found on a lake in northern Maine, high in the Rockies, on a prairie in Montana, and near the Canadian border in northernmost Idaho. The silence never lasts long, for it is soon interrupted by a distant airplane, a squirrel chattering, or a fish jumping.

Composers have tried to capture this vastness, as well as birdsong and the sounds of nature and the garden. Probably the most famous example is Beethoven's Sixth Symphony, the Pastorale. This is a marvelous evocation of a walk into the country from old Vienna on a summer's day, with the birds singing and the fresh sun glittering. But then clouds build up and cover the sun, and a thunderstorm opens in the sky, destroying serenity, pelting everything with cold rain. Just as quickly, the storm passes and the sun returns. The music rejoices in the return of life, taking us into a moment of transcendent bliss before the symphony ends.

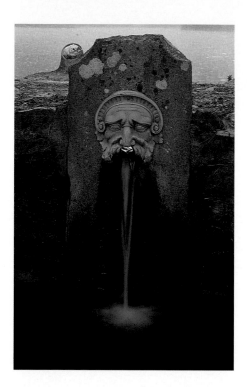

ABOVE. *An ornate waterspout creates sound in the garden of Prince Wolkonsky in Tredarzec, France. The effect of this place, and others around the water on his property, is one of age and classic beauty, although the garden was built and has been maintained by the prince himself over many years.*

OPPOSITE TOP. *Many voices issue from this grotto—a stone waterwheel in another part of Prince Wolkonsky's garden. Primroses (*Primula*) and ferns grow on the near shore. This evocative landscape is forever laughing with the sound of falling water.*

OPPOSITE BOTTOM. *Water attracts life, and life likes to sing. A pond like this one at the garden of Madame d'Andlau in Remalard, France, will attract singing birds, humming insects, and noisy frogs—who like to think they can sing. Perhaps the silent song of the stone frogs is more captivating.*

WATER'S LAUGHTER

One of the most soothing sounds in nature is the laughter of falling water. Those lucky enough to have a brook on their property may be doubly fortunate if it falls fast enough to create the burbling that seems to settle us. Otherwise, you can make a pond or a dam and send the water over the top to create the sound of falling water. Even a small pump-driven pool and watercourse can add the sound of water to a surprisingly large area.

Watercourses can be planned more for the sound they make than for their appearance. They do not have to be a simulated streambed or corny "tiki" waterfall down a stack of rocks. They can be placed in the back of the garden, out of sight, and involve a small pool of water and a recirculating pump. The water is pumped by a length of hose to the top of a water orchestra—a series of containers, stones, shells, or anything else that causes water to make a sound as it falls. I once saw one made of abalone shells, set edgewise into concrete. The water ran into the top abalone shell, where it spilled over into the shell below. The sound was symphonic.

A fountain accomplishes pretty much the same thing. While ornamented fountains can be very decorative in a formal garden, they are usually out of place in a naturalistic setting. Fountains do not have to be ornamented, however. A natural-looking small pond or pool of water can have a submerged, invisible fountain mechanism that sends up a stream of water. Streams of water do not often shoot out of ponds in wild nature, but a garden is nature improved. The recirculating water keeps the pond aerated and free of anaerobic organisms, and the sound of the water is enchanting.

Water attracts other creatures who can add to the soundscape. Frogs will eventually come to a pond, to emit their varieties of cricks and chirrups. If your pond is large, you may attract a pair or more of honking Canada geese.

INSECT MUSIC

The more diverse the plantings on your property, the more environmental niches will be available, and consequently, the more varied the inhabitants, including the insects. Some insect sounds are unpleasant—the sound of frass dropping from a tree infested with gypsy moths, for instance. But what pleasure we get from fields and trees in bloom when they are full of buzzing bees. Or a night full of crickets—the definitive sound of late summer. And katydid choruses in the late August woodlands of the eastern United States can be deafening. Water helps diversity, and with diversity comes a greater multitude of nature's voices.

This natural symphony never repeats and never ends. It is the rush and roar of all life working in interlocked splendor, but to hear it we need to be quiet.

INSTRUMENTS AND ORCHESTRAS

Natural sounds in the garden can be supplemented by human inventions, as well. Many people like wind chimes, and their sound is appropriate in a garden. Wind chimes do not have to be metal pipes that ring with bell-like tones. Various lengths of hollow bamboo hung together make deep, clunking sounds when moved by the wind, and small sticks can be hung to clatter together.

Some clever people make Aeolian harps—instruments played by the wind—for their landscapes, but these cannot be purchased, as far as I know. The name comes from Aeolus, Greek god of the winds, who gave Ulysses a fair wind and put the unfavorable winds in a bag—subsequently opened by Ulysses's men, with disastrous consequences. Originally, Aeolian harps were sound boxes with about ten strings tuned in unison, set to resonate in the prevailing wind. The concept is quite old; David, in Hebrew lore, was said to have hung his lyre about his bed at night to capture the night winds. Today the concept is applied to any device producing musical sounds from the wind. They may be long tubes that make a slow, deep hoot. They can be simple wires, strung tightly at various lengths, that sing in the wind. Or they can be powered by vanes that turn a crank that makes a sound. In modern parlance, any wind-driven, sound-making device is an Aeolian harp, and that would include wind chimes.

Gardens also make fine settings for recorded or live music. As a boy, I lived in the country. One afternoon I set my record player in an upstairs bedroom window, facing out into the yard. It was a warm summer day, and I put a recording of Handel's "Water Music" on the turntable and went to the yard to relax. Within a few minutes, I noticed about a dozen dragonflies had arrived and were swirling and swooping about in front of the window in perfect time to the music. They kept up this dance until the music stopped, and then they all flew away. We lived about a mile from the nearest watercourse. I had never seen a dragonfly on the property before, and I have never seen one since. Were they lured there to dance by Handel's genius? I have often wondered about that.

Soft music spilling into the garden from weatherproof outdoor speakers can be quite effective when the garden must be at its most elegant—although I personally prefer the natural chorus of birds above all else.

RIGHT. *Besides the natural music that occurs in gardens, gardens are natural places for listening to music. What could be a more fitting musical setting than the garden of Cecil and Molly Smith in Oregon, where Douglas firs* (Pseudotsuga menziesii) *vault overhead, trillium blooms by the stone bench, and an ornamental currant* (Ribes sanguineum) *has burst into Wagnerian pink fire in the background?*

Taste

*Yahweh God planted a garden in Eden which is in the east,
and there he put the man he had fashioned. Yahweh God
caused to spring up from the soil every kind of tree, enticing to
look at and good to eat, with the tree of life and the tree of the
knowledge of good and evil in the middle of the garden.
Yahweh God took the man and settled him in the garden of
Eden to cultivate and take care of it.*

Genesis 2:8–16

PAGES 138-139 AND ABOVE. *Out walking on one of the first chilly days of fall, on a hill with the fresh breeze in our face, luck would have us find crab apples like these growing in Shara White's garden in Bonners Ferry, Idaho. A few of their tart kisses and we are refreshed for the rest of the journey. In winter (above), memories of the scent of apple blossoms and the sweet juicy apples that followed haunt the orchard. Note how the pruning keeps the branches and leaves well-exposed to sunlight and the fruit within easy picking reach of the ground.*

OPPOSITE. *One could argue forever about which fruit tastes best, but surely among the front-runners would be ripe, luscious peaches like these (*Prunus persica *'Frost') photographed at the Jim and Katy Nollman Garden on San Juan Island in Washington.*

In this seemingly simple quote from Genesis, humankind is given its provender and its purpose. We are here to cultivate the garden and to take care of it.

Interestingly, the ancient Hebrew word for "garden" in this passage is translated as "paradise" in the Greek version. A garden is surely a form of paradise, where nature is perfected. Our notion of what makes a paradise always returns to the image of a beautiful and fruitful garden—apples fall into the hand, arbors drip with grapes, and the ground is jeweled with red berries.

The wonderful proclivity of plants to produce sweet droplets of sugar seems to be for our enjoyment alone—but only on first thought. Many animals, especially the birds, eat sweet fruit and berries, and carry the seeds far away, dispersing the plants. For many years I thought that this was the reason plants made sweet fruit—to aid in seed dispersal. But when I moved to an abandoned pear orchard, the trees' chief purpose for producing sugary fruit was made clear to me.

Each year the previous owner mowed the weeds, which dried and were burned to nothing by the fierce California sun. The little that decayed back into the soil was not nearly as much as the soil gave up to produce the weeds and grasses, and so every year the orchard soil became less fertile. For the first few years after I moved in, the pears got short shrift. I never even bothered to harvest them, and the fruit rotted where it fell, under the trees. After several years, the annual grasses grew much denser, bigger, and greener under the trees where the soil had been given a yearly mulch of sweet fruit. I remembered reading a scientific paper about the effect of a tablespoon of ordinary white sugar dissolved into every quart of water used on a test group of potted plants—it caused the soil bacteria in the pots to proliferate. They bloomed, quickly died, and decayed to feed the roots of the potted plants. Plants given sugary water grew denser, bigger, and greener.

So the sweet fruit that hangs so delectably from summer brambles, bushes, and trees is not just for us. The plants have a secret purpose all their own as they fertilize the ground in which they grow.

ABOVE. *What wealth appears on our trees when the cherries turn ripe! What king or queen could eat better than we do when we fill our pockets with ripe Bing cherries? These Bings—sweet, dark jewels of fruit— are growing in Vicky and Fred Kingsland's garden in Bonners Ferry, Idaho.*

OPPOSITE TOP. *Gardeners who grow tayberries like these at the Gianangello Herb Farm on San Juan Island in Washington get the best of both worlds, because tayberries are a cross between blackberries and raspberries with a mild flavor that resembles both parents. They also ripen earlier than most blackberries.*

OPPOSITE BOTTOM. *'Frau Dagmar Hartopp' is a hybrid rugosa rose very highly rated by the American Rose Society, with medium pink flowers and a pretty habit. As an added bonus, the flowers are followed by big, tart hips like these growing at the Bob Dash Garden on Long Island in New York.*

SUGAR IN EXCELSIS

Sweet is one of the four actual tastes (sweet, sour, salty, bitter). All other so-called tastes, such as bubble gum and pot roast, are given their character and nuance by their aromas, which waft up into the back of our nasal passages as we eat, stimulating our olfactory organs. Most of what we call taste is actually smell.

Of the four true tastes, sweet is the one we most value. We humans have a sweet tooth, and we use it to gauge a fruit's ripeness and edibility. A liking for sweet food is hard-wired into our neurological circuitry. In hunter-gatherer times, it was a survival mechanism; now it may be our downfall, as sugar is no longer scarce. The same holds true of fatty foods. We crave sugar and fat because they are the richest sources of food energy. Once scarce, requiring a trek of many miles or a lengthy hunt, sugar and fat are now as close as the corner doughnut shop.

We are better off following our sweet tooth into the garden. How delightful to wander through a landscape and find fruit growing for our delectation! It is in our hunting-gathering nature to enjoy it.

We gardeners can plan to have a little something for our visitors from spring to fall. Strawberries, of course, are one of the first fruits of spring. Main-crop strawberries are good for the vegetable garden, but in the ornamental landscape, the little fraises de bois, or alpine strawberries, are more useful. They produce no runners, their berries are richly fragrant and tasty, they produce fruit freely from spring to fall, and they will grow well and set fruit in semishade. I particularly like 'Baron Solemacher' among the red-berried sorts; the yellow variety may have the most intense fragrance of all. The best strawberry of all is the wild strawberry (*Fragaria virginiana*) of the meadows in the eastern United States. "Doubtless God could have made a better berry," wrote Izaak Walton, "but doubtless God never did." These wild berries are hard to transplant unless they really like their spot. Poor, acid soil in old meadows is a favorite site. It is no exaggeration to say that a bowl of vanilla ice cream topped with loads of freshly picked, still sun-warm wild strawberries is the food of paradise.

A stand of black currant (*Ribes nigrum*) makes a nice, thick, medium-green hedge when given full sun and well-manured, well-watered soil. It leafs out early, produces fruit early, is not prone to pests or diseases, is easily propagated by cuttings, is hardy to the coldest zones, and produces heavy fruit crops. Best of all, you can eat fresh, ripe black currants by June. Eating these purple-black berries may be an acquired taste. They are oddly scented, as are the leaves, with a musky odor. There is something of this distinctiveness in the flavor, too, although currants taste mostly like blackberries or raisins.

When one understands how packed with vitamin C these berries are, the taste is quickly acquired, and then it is a problem staying out of the currant patch. When black-currants are cooked and strained for juice, however, this musky flavor subsides. The juice may be sweetened and poured into ice-cube trays. When frozen, pop the cubes into a tightly closed freezer bag. Thaw and use for summer drinks, to add as cassis to indifferent white wine, to ladle over a lemon Bavarian or over lemon sherbet. In paradise, this is the dessert that is served when they run out of strawberries and ice cream.

What is a black currant without a red currant nearby? These cultivated varieties of *Ribes sativum* also produce heavy, trouble-free crops of early red berries, but they are sour until they hang on the bush for weeks, eventually turning a deeper, clear red. Then they are bursting with sweet juice. The variety 'Red Lake' has always produced well for me, but there are other varieties with white as well as red fruit. The currants, like their relatives the thorny gooseberry and the hybrid Jostaberry (half black currant and half gooseberry), need a yearly thinning out of all canes and branches three or more years old. This thinning keeps fruit production high and the plants young and healthy looking.

In the warm zones, citrus fruits become possible for gardeners. Few trees look as inviting as a dark green navel orange, with its bottom branches removed to show its ornamental trunk, dotted with bright orange fruit. The more delectable the citrus, it seems, the less hardy it is. In Zone 9, Meyer lemons are reliably hardy, unless a particularly harsh winter occurs.

Grapes are as beautiful as they

are delicious. The French and Italians are fond of running them up and over the farmhouse door. Grapevines easily cover an outdoor trellis; they may also be trained along a fence, or even stand alone by themselves when their trunk becomes thick enough to support the top weight. Grapes naturally climb and play in the branches of trees, and there is no reason not to allow cultivated varieties to do the same thing. Use a semidwarf fruit tree or small ornamental—about ten to fifteen feet (3 to 4.5 meters) tall at most—or you will need a ladder to get the grapes. Prune the grapevine back to just thirty to sixty buds, depending on the vigor of the plant; the more vigorous it is, the more buds you leave. Hard pruning to fewer buds will increase the vigor of a weaker vine, and consequently the new shoots will grow longer. Grapevines can also be trained to grow up a garden shed, pergola, or other structure. Best of all, construct a wooden trellis or fence specifically for fruiting vines and run the garden path alongside them, so that when they are ripe, visitors will be tempted to swipe a bunch to eat as they walk. Among the tastiest varieties are Canadice, Gewurztraminer, Steuben, Alden, Einset, and Concord. Alden is uniquely delicious, hardy to Zone 5, but prone to diseases and pests. Gewurztraminer—ordinarily used for making white wine—is probably the best wine grape of all for eating out of hand. It is sweetly, spicily, fragrantly floral.

Both for flowers and fruit, you may want an apple tree or two; keep them to semidwarf or dwarf sizes so they will not dominate the landscape, and so that you will be able to reach the top of the trees not only to harvest, but to thin and manage the crop. Smaller trees also make it easier to control any pest outbreaks that may occur and provide more apples suitable for eating. A slightly more original approach is to plant a grove of bitter, tannic English cider apples from the wonderfully named varieties such as Kingston Black, Porter's Perfection, Foxwhelp, Tremblett's Bitter, Yarlington Mill, and Grindstone. Add some of this fruit to the harvest from the sweet apple trees, varieties like Cox's Orange Pippin, Gravenstein, Winesap, Smokehouse, Northern Spy, and others. The result will be marvelous cider for a cold October night.

For an intriguing look, plant a dwarf apple variety and grow a clematis up into its branches. Underplant with a shrub or two to shade the Clematis stem near the ground. The vine will work its way out into the sunlight and decorate the tree with large clematis flowers.

Pears, like apples, make perfect yard fruit. Every Pennsylvania Dutch farmhouse seems to have its seckel pear planted out in the front yard. Bartletts grow well and set big crops, but they cannot compare in flavor to Comice. In years when the fruit is bug-bitten or misshapen, you can make pear cider, or perry. Or add pears to the apple cider.

Peaches are heavenly, but prone to diseases and insects. Apricots are pretty trees, but in most places they bloom too early: the blossoms freeze, destroying any potential for a crop. In the years when the trees do set crops, the fruit may be taken by brown rot before it ripens.

Plums are pretty in bloom and usually fairly trouble free. The Italian prune plums are meaty, tasty, and can be dried for prunes. Japanese plums are graceful in form, but their fruits are small. The Santa Rosa plum is an excellent variety for eating and is tidy in the yard.

Blueberries are handsome plants. They make pretty screens, hedges, or borders, growing to just about six feet (1.8 meters) tall and not quite as big around. There are a few strictly ornamental sorts, but why plant them, when you can have a good-looking bush that produces fat, juicy blueberries?

The brambles—raspberries, blackberries, and their relatives—are not particularly pretty, but that matters little when their cane tips are drooping from their loads of sweet fruit. Raspberries—black, red, yellow, white, and purple; blackberries and their kin the boysenberries and ollalaberries; the luscious wineberry (*Rubus phoenicolasius*): blessings on all their tribe. Brambles can be planted in out-of-the-way corners of the garden, to be discovered

OPPOSITE. *Rowan (*Sorbus aucuparia*) berries hang undisturbed on a tree at Wayside Gardens in Creston, Canada. Although birds will eat them, humans find these berries unpalatable. For the last few years before his death in 1926, Luther Burbank was working to produce sorbus trees with large, tasty fruits. At the remnants of his farm in Sebastopol, California, one can still see sorbus trees with fruit the size of hen's eggs, but with the same bitter, unpalatable flavor. Burbank had gotten them to size, and was working to improve the flavor when he died.*

perchance, or not, as the luck of the visitor would have it. The gardener for sure will make a path to the ripe berry patch. I discovered my first patch of wild wineberries at that wonderful age made just for exploring: eleven years old. I had wandered that summer day to the hills around my home in the Pocono mountains. Just above a creek and dam, and just below a stand of pine, was a thick patch of wineberries laden with ripe fruit. I could not believe my good fortune and stuffed myself with the reddish orange, sunwarmed, raspberry-like fruit. In my paradise is a patch of wineberries.

In Eden there must be a cherry tree, with rich, red fruits hanging in pairs, waiting for someone to gobble them up. But then in Eden there must be no cherry-loving birds. To salvage cherries before the birds eat them, one must sleep with the lights on. Robins, especially, will eat some, peck holes in others, and sometimes just slash at them. Bing cherries are standard and really unsurpassed for flavor and texture. Black Tartarian comes in a close second, along with Emperor Francis—a yellow and reddish cherry. All sweet cherries are prone to brown rot, however.

Then there are the exotics: the banana-custard–flavored pawpaw (*Asimina triloba*); the fruity-to-the-point-of-nausea mayapple (*Podophyllum peltatum*); the jujube (*Ziziphus jujuba*) from China; the hanson bush cherry (*Prunus tomentosa*); the trailing dewberry; the fruit of *Cornus mas;* elderberries (*Sambucus canadensis*), wild cherry (*Prunus serotina*); rose hips, and many others.

SALADS AND SAVORIES

While sweet fruits have heavenly flavors, they are only the beginning of what the garden has to offer. A good ear of corn is sweet, not fruity—but no less than wonderful. Fresh salad greens are an intriguing mixture of bitter and sweet. In the garden with a skep, or beehive, rich honey—the concentrated essence of a million sunstruck flowers—drips in the honeycomb.

Human know-how can transform the products of the garden and orchard into passionately flavored substances like wine—grape juice elevated by the lowly yeast to an elixir, kissed by the scent of the oak tree, and stored away in a cool, dark place, eventually to emerge as bottled poetry. Other tastes tend toward the less ethereal: earthy, like mushrooms; resinous, like rosemary; herbal, like oregano; imitative, like lemon thyme.

It is the herbs in our kitchen garden, in fact, that infuse many of our favorite dishes with their superb flavors. These same plants are often beautiful enough to be worthy specimens for our most careful landscapes. Their leaf textures, foliage colors, and softly beautiful flowers, displayed in drifts or as border plantings, walkway edgings, or (with mother-of-thyme) in the cracks between the paving stones, serve double duty.

I found out how valuable a good stand of thyme is after a trip to Italy, where I discovered a dish called "Pollo Sciacciata"—pressed chicken. Handfuls of thyme are placed on a hot grill, then the whole chicken, cut through the back and breast so it can be splayed open, is placed on the thyme and covered with a heavy weight. The thyme burns and sears the chicken. After eight minutes or so, the grill is cleared, fresh thyme put down, and the chicken turned over and weighted down again. The result is magnificent.

The rich bronze to reddish black leaves of opal basil rival *Heuchera* 'Palace Purple' for leaf color; this variety has the extra advantage of being useful in cooking and salads.

Edible flowers for salads or for garnishes include the little blue flowers of rosemary, which add an herbal note to a salad. The blue flowers of society garlic (*Tulbaghia violacea*) are so intensely flavored of garlic that one floret is all you need in an entire salad. Impatiens flowers are edible—although not particularly flavorful—and add color to a salad. The flowers of nasturtium, both in bud and in full-blown blossom, are spicy, tangy, delicious, and colorful. Pineapple sage (*Salvia elegans*) flowers are bright crimson and beautify salads and garnish sherbets. Borage flowers are a clear, watery blue and taste like cucumbers. Calendula has a mild, vegetable-like taste, and its petals add a rich orange-yellow color to salads or can serve as garnishes for dishes like baked fish. Other edible flowers include the petals of daylilies, chrysanthemums, violet flowers, yucca, pansy, tulip, and gladiolus; carnations, lavender, marigolds, hollyhocks, and honeysuckle. Rose petals are edible, and garnishes are made with lilac, red clover, bee balm,

ABOVE. *The sensuous curves of garlic are captured in the photographer's garden in Bonners Ferry, Idaho.*

OPPOSITE TOP. *Famed plantswoman Rosemary Verey expertly uses the ornamental possibilities of food crops in this portion of her garden at Barnsley House in Gloucestershire, England. A planting of red-leaf lettuce is interplanted with 'Red Drumhead' cabbage with great effect in this small bed.*

OPPOSITE BOTTOM. *Ornamental amaranth grows at Wave Hill in the Bronx, New York. Amaranth's wild cousin is the ordinary redroot pigweed commonly found in fields and gardens. It also produces a high-protein seed that the Aztec Indians called "the food of the gods." It is quite nutty and crunchy, and can be popped like popcorn. Modern amaranth breeding has succeeded in developing this plant as both a promising food crop and an ornamental for visual beauty.*

ABOVE. *Cabbages grow among purple lobelia and golden calendula flowers in the winter garden at Calloway Gardens in Pine Mountain, Georgia. While the lobelia is not edible, the petals of calendula flowers are often used to brighten winter salads in warm regions of the country.*

OPPOSITE. *Mint grows below* Rosa rugosa, *which will later produce edible hips, and* Alchemilla mollis *at Hadspen Garden in Somerset, England. A stand of mint to refresh the taste should be situated in every garden—but keep it confined, for mint tends to grow rampantly in moist soil.*

English daisy, fuchsia, and apple and elderberry blossoms.

The most complete culinary herb gardens contain thyme, oregano, parsley, summer and winter savories, basil, borage, chervil, chives, coriander (cilantro), dill, fennel, garlic, mint, rosemary, shallots, French tarragon, and sage. Many of these herbs have several useful varieties. Sage, for instance, comes in common garden forms, but also in varieties with variegated yellow or purple leaves, and in tall forms such as pineapple sage. Basil comes in several leaf colors. Two bright new basil cultivars are the blue-green 'African Blue' and the large-leaved 'Burgundy Beauty'.

The Mediterranean herbs, with the volatile oils in the leaves and heavy scents (primarily rosemary, sage, oregano, and thyme), produce their most aromatic leaves in poor, dry soils, and so make a good choice for such spots on the property. Most of the other herbs like good garden soil with a constant supply of moisture. Rosemary is being improved; there are new cultivars like 'Madeline Hill', which is both hardier and prettier than the common rosemary.

As for working edible plantings into the landscape, this is where agriculture gets to be fun. Chives, parsley, beets, and carrots make fine edgings for walkways and flower gardens. Lettuces come in many forms and colors, as do the ornamental curly kales. New Zealand spinach makes a good ground cover in sunny spots.

Peppers, both sweet and hot, make pretty ornamental plants because of their leaves and forms.

Eggplants have flowers as pretty as any in the garden, and the black-purple fruits combine well with white, pink, orange, and red flowers. The bright red stalks of red or rhubarb chard make striking vertical accents, especially in a colorful border of annuals. Okra can be planted at the back of the border, for its pretty flowers will accent lower-growing sorts of herbaceous flowering plants, especially perennials such as white and blue *Platycodon*s. Among the most ornamental of vegetables is the globe artichoke, with its gray-green, spiny leaves. It can be grown successfully as far north as New England if it is carefully wintered over or grown as an annual by being given an early start inside.

DESIGN FOR FLAVOR

On a visit to France, I went with a good gardener to what he called his special garden. He showed me to the edge of what looked like an overgrown weed patch. We went into the weed patch, and I, singularly unimpressed, wondered if he was crazy. "Look around at the plants," he said. I started looking closely and soon found that every plant there produced a fruit, seed, nut, edible leaf, or edible root. The wasted looking weeds were the tops of potatoes dying down. The small, bushy trees were dwarf fruit trees of all kinds. Grapes and squashes grew rampantly into them. The ground was littered with squash vines, strawberry plants, and other low-growers. The weeds that grew everywhere turned out to be fennel, dill, chervil, chives, and tarragon.

This man could garden, but his goal was high yield rather than a smart appearance; his special garden was a jumble of plants, unappealing to me. How much nicer when edible plants are worked into good landscape designs! Here are a few of my guidelines for using edible plants in the landscape.

• Use herbs as you would any annual, biennial, or perennial, mixed into perennial beds or borders.

• Use small fruit trees as individual specimens on low pedestals or in featured places.

• Group semidwarf fruit trees in odd-numbered groups to form small groves into which the visitor can wander. Plant so that the canopies of the trees touch, which forces them

upwards; prune the lowest branches so that walking under the trees is easy and they form a continuous canopy overhead.

• Use hazelnuts (filberts) as a screening hedge; these plants make thick stands of tall, many-trunked, woody trees.

• Keep fruit trees away from decks and patios; the fruit drops and will turn mushy and discolor the surface. The exception is a grapevine over a doorway, on a pergola, and within easy reach of someone on the patio.

• If the house is situated at the top of a steep hill, plant fragrant apple trees on the hillside so that sun-warmed spring air will catch their scent and waft it up to the house.

• Edge walkways with blueberries, huckleberries, strawberries, and currants—it is fun to pick and eat them as you walk. Avoid lining walkways with thorny plants like gooseberries, raspberries, and blackberries. These should be approached on purpose, in their lair, with caution in mind and the knowledge that picking their fruit requires some resignation to dealing with thorns.

• Plant a row of scented geraniums along a walkway within easy reach of passersby, so that they can discover the delightful scents of these leaves: apple, lemon, lime, rose, cinnamon, and many others.

• Keep a culinary herb and kitchen vegetable garden close to the kitchen door, in a sunny spot. Raised beds look nicest, and the paths between them can be easily maintained if they are planted with lawn grass.

• Plant some purely ornamental plants in every edible garden, and some edible plants in every ornamental garden. Use the ornamental qualities of edible plants: strawberries as good ground covers, rhubarb for a big-leaved statement, well-shaped fruit trees as star attractions, squash shading an exposed bank from the sun, grapes and late roses intertwined on a trellis.

• Plant hot chiles in pots for the sunny porch. Their fiery red fruits are ornamental, and you will have them close at hand to add zest to your cooking.

• Plant much more thyme (ordinary *Thymus vulgaris*) than you ever think you will need, for once you start using it by the handful on the barbeque grill, you will soon need all you can find.

• Make a small lawn of chamomile. It is drought-resistant, soft, and wonderfully fragrant, and it substitutes well for grass; can also be used as tea.

• Plant passionfruit vines to twine along porch railings so the fruit is at hand when ripe.

• Plant asparagus in drifts along the back of the perennial border, in a spot where the plants are easily accessible. Their soft fern looks beautiful behind lower-growing, coarser, summer-blooming perennials such as *Campanula glomerata*.

A garden with something delicious to eat tucked into it is a more human place, a friendlier place, than a garden of ornamentals alone. But there is one taste that plants cannot provide: the taste of pure springwater.

My last property had a springhouse located in the woods behind the main house. Stone steps led down to a sandy-bottomed pool of clear, flowing springwater. Kneeling there, I daily dipped my lips onto the surface of the water and drank. The taste was icy, sweet, delicious. Not every property, of course, will have such a spring, but every property can have a drinking fountain somewhere near the garden where thirst can be quenched and the body refreshed, while the garden does the same thing for the soul.

OPPOSITE. *A path winds between clumps of tall ornamental onions (*Allium giganteum*) at the Van Dusen Botanical Garden in Vancouver, Canada. In the foreground are smaller clumps of chives (*Allium schoenoprasum*). Alliums both purely ornamental and edible are useful in bringing the food and flower gardens together.*

The Sixth Sense

O mickle is the powerful grace that lies
In plants, herbs, stones, and their true qualities.
William Shakespeare

The sixth sense is the one that perceives a reality beyond the material world. Through it we receive hints of the true meaning of the world around us, and in its light we begin to see the value of events and objects. The sixth sense brings us the premonitory dream. It alerts us that something is wrong when nothing appears to be wrong, and that everything is all right when nothing appears to be right at all. It guides us from a higher (or perhaps deeper) perspective.

The sixth sense is the key to living an artful life, for an artful life—graceful, compassionate, well timed—can not be arranged. To live artfully, one must trust what one feels through all the senses, especially the sixth. The eyes are subject to illusion: a chemical may taste like a strawberry; we often hear things incorrectly. When deep feelings occur and urge us forward, however, we had best follow or be prepared to interrupt the flow of heaven. An artful life is not achieved by planning but emerges as a person follows his or her heart.

Intuition is the prompting we receive from this higher or deeper realm through the sixth sense. A strong and trusted intuition is a particularly great help in gardening, where we most often work with what will be, not what is. We put in small seedlings or started plants, envisioning how they will look when they are grown. We site plants based on our knowledge of their needs, but we also intuit where they will thrive.

In fact, the chief joy of gardening is being able to use intuition to create beauty. In my front garden there was a blank space between clumps of daylilies and some tall, spring-blooming shrubs. Just to the left of the blank space, a clump of angelica grew. I stared at it for a while

---

PAGES 152-153. *A beautiful garden can stimulate thoughts of what could be, or what might have been. Given a quiet, private hour in a garden like Rosemary Verey's at Barnsley House in Gloucestershire, England, some stirring of the soul will surely occur.*

RIGHT. *Nature is profligate in her beauty, be it vast or even small. The exquisite form of sycamore* (Acer pseudoplatanus) *leaves and flowers demonstrates to our sixth sense that the creative force of the world lavishes beauty on even the most humble things, and thankfully gives human beings a unique sense to appreciate it. This branch was photographed at the garden of Mr. and Mrs. Andrew Norton at East Lambrook Manor near South Petherton, England.*

ABOVE. *A gardener is the spirit of the garden, the organizing force, the heart and soul of it all. Even when absent from his garden, Prince Wolkonsky's vision and work remain.*

when suddenly the word *"Ligularia"* popped into my head. I did not know too much about this perennial at the time, so I looked it up in my reference works. It fit the site perfectly: partial shade; rich, moist soil. It produces large, orange, daisylike flowers in the late summer and early fall, continuing the color scheme begun by the daylilies in June and continued by the shrubs—a yellow and red *Hibiscus rosa-sinensis* and a lighter yellow *Potentilla fruticosa.* It could not have been a better choice. Even though I was not familiar with *Ligularia dentata* 'Othello', it suggested itself to me, and stars in that spot to this day.

Humans have developed a sixth sense where the natural world is concerned, because for most of our history as a species, our survival has depended on knowing nature's ways intuitively. Once I was reading about chanterelle mushrooms—the delicious ones the color of egg yolks that appear in spring and fall. Suddenly, an image of a woods I knew about forty miles away came into my mind. "That's where I'll find chanterelles," I said to myself. In an hour, I was parking the car and beginning the half-mile walk through fields and marshes to get to the woods. When I entered their canopy, the forest floor was a carpet of chanterelle mushrooms!

The garden setting also prompts flashes of insight into the nature of things. As the little placards say, "One is nearer God's heart in a garden than anywhere else on earth." And in God's heart are kept the secrets of things: why the nocturnal owl hoots while its diurnal relative,

the hawk, screams; why the waxy-petaled flowers smell so good; why the grass has one cotyledon while most other plants have two.

At the heart of life lie mysteries. We can see many things clearly, but not ourselves. What is this blind self-awareness that suffuses us? How did we get caught up in the flow of time? What relationship do we have with the animals and plants that inhabit this world with us?

Sitting in a garden, it is not hard to believe that we and the plants are part of a greater whole that includes us all. We animals are implicit—our roots are folded into our bellies, where we take nourishment from the plants we eat. The plants are explicit—taking nourishment from the soil into which their roots are sunk.

In the realm of the mind, it may also be the same. Animals are implicit—our consciousness is folded into us, creating the illusion of separateness. Plants are explicit—their consciousness is not located within an organ, but is the consciousness that resides explicitly in the world. It is the intelligence that turns the face of the flower to the sun, that creates the barbs on the cocklebur that catch the hair of animals.

Whether implicit or explicit, as the prophet Isaiah said, "All flesh is grass." All life is connected. We are part of our gardens, and our gardens are a part of us.

And so our lives are reflected in the garden. We have seen the excitement of childhood, full of hope and promise, in the first sunny days of spring, when the seedlings and tightly balled knots of leaves come tentatively forth out of the moist earth.

We have felt the sensuous sexual urges of youth in the June garden, full of heady scents and wildly colored flowers just begging for love and fulfillment. We have relished the sweaty days of high summer when the plants set fruit and the cycles are renewed, and the cultivation of the garden is in our hands. We have relaxed into the soft, warm days of autumn, packed with the ripe fruits of our labors, with days like rich, red wines that make us giddy with delight. We have stood silently in the cold, gray November afternoons as the garden's dried leaves and dead stalks rattled in the wind, and the small birds chased each other through the bare bushes. And we have seen the dead of winter, frozen, immobile, and yet clear, because death has been experienced, transcended, and the garden is pure, bright, shining potential.

We are fortunate to be alive. Each of our senses is a gift from the whole to the part—from the universe to us—through which we end our isolation and know what mothers us. In our gardens, our senses detect the kind, gentle, and understanding nature of the world. Flowers, leaves, vines, branches, trunks, roots, and fruits surround us, weaving us into their fabric. There is no garden without a gardener. We belong in the picture. We are as essential as the rain and the sun.

Our senses tell us that in the garden we are home and we are loved.

ABOVE. *Prince Wolkonsky has set his garden in motion toward the ideal, and once begun, the impetus is ever forward.*

PAGES 158-159. *The perfect plants to frame the perfect doorway in the garden of our dreams:* Rosa 'Ramona', *on the left,* Ceanothus impressus, *on the right, and the pink* Rhaphiolepsis indica *flanking the path of cobbles and concrete. Some would call it heaven on earth, and by that they mean that beauty is stimulating their sixth sense, and they feel a vast presence somewhere behind the surface of things.*

PAGE 160. *Our tour of the garden of the senses is finished. The gate is closed for now. But though we are absent for a time, or are busy with the mundane things of the world, the garden waits for our visit, full of flowers, ready to please when we are ready for pleasure.*

Appendices

CHART OF PLANTS BY SENSUOUS QUALITIES

Note: Page numbers in italics indicate photographs

PLANT	COMMON NAME	SENSE	ZONE	DESCRIPTION	PAGE
Annuals					
Brassica oleracea	Wild Cabbage	**SO**		The ancestor of our garden *brassicas*, including cabbage, broccoli, cauliflower, collards, kale, and more	*133*
Cosmos bipinnatus	Cosmos	**S/C**		Many-branched stems with small leaves and large daisy-like flowers in rose, lavender, purple, crimson, and pink	*38, 43*
Impatiens biflora	Impatiens	**S/C, T, TA**		Small clumping plants with neat, intensely-colored little flowers in white, pink, reds	*49,* 118–20, 147
Lavatera trimestris	Annual Mallow	**S/C**		3- to 6-ft. (91.4-cm to 1.8-m) hedging plants with satiny, 4-in. (10.2-cm) flowers in white, pink, and rose	*42*
Matthiola incana	Stock	**SM**		Winter or cool season biennial grown as an annual for its sweetly fragrant blue to white, yellow, or red-purple flowers	85, 101–3, 111
Matthiola longipetala bicornis	Evening Scented Stock	**SM**		Purple flowers closed by day, but at night open to perfume the air with a heady fragrance	105
Myosotis sylvatica	Forget-Me-Not	**S/C**		Loose stems make mounds of soft, hairy leaves covered in late winter and spring with little blue flowers with white eyes	37, 41, 49
Reseda odorata	Mignonette	**SM**		Open, sprawling plants with small clusters of exquisitely fragrant greenish-yellow flowers	103, 111

S=SIGHT S/C=SIGHT/COLOR S/F=SIGHT/FORM S/L=SIGHT/LINE SM=SMELL T=TOUCH SO=SOUND TA=TASTE *=6TH SENSE

PLANT	COMMON NAME	SENSE	ZONE	DESCRIPTION	PAGE
Bulbs and Corms					
Amaryllis belladonna	Naked Ladies	**SM**	8	Makes large group of straplike leaves in winter and spring; foliage dies by summer; fragrant pink flowers appear on 2-ft. (61-cm) stalks in late summer	87, 105
Begonia 'Red Picotee'	Tuberous Begonia	**S/C**	10	Tubers planted in spring make pretty mounds of leaves with white and red-edged flowers in summer to fall	36
Canna	Canna Lilies	**S/C**	10	Tuberous tropical plants that produce large banana-like leaves and flowers in reds, yellows, apricot, coral, salmon, etc., on 4- to 6-ft. (1.2 to 1.8-m) stalks	52
Crinum moorei	Crinum	**SM**	9	Persistent sword-shaped leaves produce several lily-like pink, fragrant blossoms in late spring or summer	88, 98
Endymion hispanicus	Spanish Bluebells	**SM**	3	1-ft. (30.5-cm) long slender leaves emerge in early spring, followed by scapes hung with many little blue bells	*101*
Erythronium americanum	Trout Lily	**T**	4	Mottled greenish-brown elongated oval leaves are chief feature; flowers brownish-yellow in early spring	118
Fritillaria meleagris	Checkered Fritillary	**S/F, S/L**	3	Impossibly checkered, blocky hanging bells emerge above small clump of slender leaves in early spring	*64*, 72
Lilium auratum	Gold-Band Lily	**SM**	3	4- to 6-ft. (1.2 to 1.8-m) plants with fragrant white lilies spotted crimson appearing in late summer to early fall	100
Lilium candidum	Madonna Lilies	**SM**	3	Clusters of upturned, 4-in. (10.2-cm), trumpet-shaped white flowers on 2- to 4-ft. (61-cm to 1.2-m) plants in June and July	100–101
Lilium formosanum		**SO**	3	5-ft. (1.5-m) plants with long, white, late-blooming flowers	*131*
Lilium longiflorum	Easter Lily	**SM**	8	Short 1- to 3-ft. (30.5 to 91.4-cm) plants produce early, fragrant, showy white trumpets	100–101
Muscari botryoides	Grape Hyacinth	**SM**	3	Standard medium-blue clusters of tiny bells resemble grape clusters that dangle on 6- to 12-in. (15.2 to 30.5-cm) stems	100
Narcissus jonquilla	Jonquil	**SM**	4	Close relative of daffodil with slender leaves, small fragrant flowers in yellow, orange, white in March-April	87, 90, 103
Tulbaghia violacea	Society Garlic	**TA**	9	Makes large clumps of long, slender leaves and airy balls of garlicky light lavender florets	147

S=SIGHT S/C=SIGHT/COLOR S/F=SIGHT/FORM S/L=SIGHT/LINE SM=SMELL T=TOUCH SO=SOUND TA=TASTE *=6TH SENSE

PLANT	COMMON NAME	SENSE	ZONE	DESCRIPTION	PAGE
Tulipa hybrids	Tulip	**S/C, S/L, SM, TA**	4	Several divisions of tulips separate varied characteristics, but all have low clump of leaves and produce flowers atop stems in various colors.	49, 72, *91*, 101, 147
'Angelique'		**S/C**	4	Double tulip with cream base, pink edges, and deep pink centers	*27*
'Gudoshnik'		**S/C**		Red and orange	*41*
'Maureen'		**S/C, S/F**		White	*35*, 61
'Red Emperor'		**S/C**		Fiery red	41

Climbers and Vines

PLANT	COMMON NAME	SENSE	ZONE	DESCRIPTION	PAGE
Anredera cordifolia	Madiera Vine	**SM**	9	1-ft. (30.5-cm) long clusters of fragrant white flowers hang from the dense evergreen foliage of this vine in fall.	97
Beaumontia grandiflora	Easter Lily Vine	**SM**	9	A 30-ft. (9.1-m) evergreen vine with large leaves and big, fragrant white blooms from spring to fall	95
Celastrus scandens	American Bittersweet	**S/C**	5	The flowers are not notable, but in the fall orange and red seedpods make a colorful display	38
Clematis armandii	Evergreen Clematis	**SM**	7	Small star-shaped fragrant flowers cluster among the narrow evergreen leaves in early spring	94–95
Clematis 'Dr. Ruppel'		**S/C**	4	A vigorous large-flowered hybrid with 8 ruffled sepals and wide carmine bars, flowering in May and June	*52*
Clematis heracleifolia		**S/C**	5	Coarse deciduous sub-shrub 4-ft. (1.2-m) tall with half-woody stems and blue hyacinth-like flowers in July and August	42
Clematis heracleifolia var. *davidiana*		**SM**	5	Herbaceous stems form a 4-ft. (1.2-m) clump with very fragrant pale to deep blue flowers in July and August	98
Clematis 'Mme. Edouard Andre'		**S/F**	4	Deciduous vine reaches 7 to 8 ft. (2.1 to 2.4 m) with deep wine-red sepals and cream-colored stamens	66
Clematis montana var. *rubens*		**S/L, SM**	3	Classic foliage and rose-mauve lightly scented flowers	*68*, 94
Clematis 'Nelly Moser'		**SM**	4	Large-flowered hybrid to 8 ft. (2.4 m) with rose-mauve sepals and red bars	*96*
Clematis paniculata	Sweet Autumn Clematis	**SM, SO**	5	Vigorous, tall climber with fragrant white flowers borne in clouds over whole vine in fall	97, 111, 130
Clematis recta var. *mandshurica*		**SM**	6	An herbaceous climber with panicles of fragrant white flowers in mid-summer	98

S=SIGHT   S/C=SIGHT/COLOR   S/F=SIGHT/FORM   S/L=SIGHT/LINE   SM=SMELL   T=TOUCH   SO=SOUND   TA=TASTE   ✳=6TH SENSE

PLANT	COMMON NAME	SENSE	ZONE	DESCRIPTION	PAGE
Decumaria barbara	Climbing Hydrangea Vine	SM	6	Fragrant flowers resemble those of a small hydrangea; white blooms appear in June and July	96
Gelsemium sempervirens	Carolina Yellow Jessamine	SM	7	Evergreen vine to 20 ft. (6.1 m) with fine leaves giving dainty appearance; fragrant yellow trumpets in late winter	94
Hedera helix	English Ivy	T	4	Familiar evergreen ivy for covering walls	*123*
Hoya carnosa	Wax Flower	SM	10	Choice potted vine, keeps to 10 ft. (3 m) and produces fragrant clusters of waxy-white stars among evergreen, leathery leaves in summer	96, 105
Jasminum grandiflorum	Royal Jasmine	SM	7	Clusters of small flowers with jasmine fragrance open all summer on shrubby-looking semi-evergreen vines	87, 96
Jasminum officinale	Poet's Jasmine	SM	7	This is the jasmine of perfumes, with small fragrant white flowers March to November on feathery-leaved vine	94
Jasminum nitidum	Angel-Wing Jasmine	SM	10	A shrubby little vine with glossy evergreen foliage and star-burst fragrant white flowers May to August	96
Jasminum polyanthum	Pink Jasmine	SM	9	Panicles of fragrant pink flowers open among dark evergreen leaves in late winter to spring	94
Jasminum sambac	Arabian Jasmine	SM	10	A shrubby evergreen vine with powerfully fragrant white flowers used in perfume and to make jasmine tea	87
Lathyrus odoratus	Sweet Pea	SM		A spring and summer annual vine with clusters of pea-like flowers available in many colors carrying a clean, sweet fragrance	100
Lonicera hildebrandiana	Giant Burmese Honeysuckle	SM	10	A big vine with 6-in. (15.2-cm) fragrant flower tubes that turn orange-red after opening white in June	96
Lonicera japonica	Japanese Honeysuckle	SM	4	Fragrant, June-blooming flowers are white with purplish tinge on oval-leaved rampant vines	88, *95*
Lonicera japonica 'Halliana'	Hall's Honeysuckle	SM	4	Familiar rampant vine evergreen in south with fragrant white and yellow flowers in late spring and summer	96
Lonicera periclymenum	Woodbine Honeysuckle	SM	4	Fragrant yellow whorled flowers with purplish markings appear along stems of this deciduous vine in summer	96
Mandevilla 'Alice duPont'		SM	10	A very compact, pretty vine with rumply leaves and gorgeous pure pink morning glory-like flowers June to November	*111*

S=SIGHT S/C=SIGHT/COLOR S/F=SIGHT/FORM S/L=SIGHT/LINE SM=SMELL T=TOUCH SO=SOUND TA=TASTE ✱=6TH SENSE

PLANT	COMMON NAME	SENSE	ZONE	DESCRIPTION	PAGE
Mandevilla laxa	Chilean Jasmine	**SM**	9	Vines have long, heart-shaped, deciduous leaves and produce fragrant clusters of ruffled white trumpets in June and July	96–97, 111
Passiflora x *alatocaerulea*	Hybrid Passionflower	**SM, T**	8	Showy, fragrant, 4-in. (10.2-cm), white and rose flowers with blue-purple crowns open all summer	97, 121
Rosa banksiae 'Lutea'	Lady Banks Rose	**S/C, S/F**	7	Long, thornless, arching green stems covered with pale yellow masses of scentless small flowers in spring	48, *57*
Rosa 'Don Juan'		**SM, SO**	8	Large, deep red roses on climbing stems perfume the air with strong damask scent from June to September	88, 130
Stephanotis floribunda	Madagascar Jasmine	**SM**	10	Dark green, glossy, leathery evergreen foliage is adorned with clusters of waxy-white, sweetly scented flowers from June to October.	96
Trachelospermum asiaticum	Yellow Star Jasmine	**SM**	8	Whitish-yellow, fragrant blossoms hang under shrubby, evergreen, climbing stems from April to July	95
Trachelospermum jasminoides	Star Jasmine	**SM**	9	Sprays of heavily jasmine-scented stars cluster profusely among attractive, dark, evergreen leaves on shrubby stems	86, 87, 95, 111
Wisteria floribunda 'Longissima'	Japanese Wisteria	**SM**	4	3-ft. (91.4-cm) clusters of fragrant, violet flowers hang from twisting, woody stems reaching 35 ft. (10.7 m).	96
Wisteria floribunda 'Longissima Alba'	White Japanese Wisteria	**SM**	4	Fragrant white clusters 15- to 24-in. (38.1 to 61-cm) long	96
Wisteria floribunda 'Rosea'	Pink Japanese Wisteria	**SM**	4	Very fragrant, 18-in. (45.7-cm) pink-flower clusters	96
Wisteria sinensis	Chinese Wisteria	**S/C, SM, SO**	5	The familiar wisteria with clusters of blue-violet, slightly fragrant flowers on huge vines to 100 ft. (30.5 m)	41, 85, 88, *91*, *95*, 96, 111, 130

Perennials

PLANT	COMMON NAME	SENSE	ZONE	DESCRIPTION	PAGE
Acanthus mollis	Bear's-Breech	**S/C, S/F**	8	Makes clumps of large, dark green, shiny leaves with hooded mauve flowers on tall spikes in summer	49, 60
Achillea taygetea 'Moonshine'		**S/C**	2	Same as species, but flowers fade to a spectacularly beautiful pale yellow	41
Aconitum napellus	Monkshood	**S/C**	2	A dark green, back border plant with 3- to 4-ft. (91.4-cm to 1.2-m) deep blue flowers in July and August	37, 44, 49
Adiantum pedatum	Five-Finger Fern	**T**	4	A choice fern whose fresh, graceful fronds split into fingers atop thin wiry stems	126

S=SIGHT S/C=SIGHT/COLOR S/F=SIGHT/FORM S/L=SIGHT/LINE SM=SMELL T=TOUCH SO=SOUND TA=TASTE ✳=6TH SENSE

PLANT	COMMON NAME	SENSE	ZONE	DESCRIPTION	PAGE
Aethionema grandiflorum	Persian Stonecress	T	3	Blue-green, fine leaves with pink umbels of tiny florets in April and May	*121*
Agapanthus orientalis	Nile Lily	S/F	9	Bulbs with 2- to 3-ft. (61 to 91.4-cm) straplike leaves bear balls of blue flowers atop thin stalks in spring and summer	60
Ajuga reptans	Bugleweed	S/C, S/F	2	Little, deep blue flower spikes arise from 6-in. (15.2-cm) creeping mats of dark green foliage in May and June	52, *57*, 60
Alchemilla mollis	Lady's Mantle	S/C, TA	3	Fan-shaped grey-green leaves with foamy sprays of small chartreuse flowers in early summer	38, *149*
Allium aflatunense		SM	4	Rosette of straplike leaves makes a 4-in. (10.2-cm) ball of lilac florets atop thick, hollow stalk in May and June	*106*
Allium giganteum	Giant Allium	TA	4	Like *A. aflatunense*, but with 5-in. (12.7-cm), bright lilac flower balls to 4 ft. (1.2 m) tall in June and July	*151*
Allium schoenoprasum	Chives	TA	4	Slender, onion flavored clumps of foliage and small blue or white flower balls in early summer	148, *151*
Allium sphaerocephalum	Drumsticks	S/C, SM	4	Dense dark red-purple balls of tightly-packed florets on 2-ft. (61-cm) stems in May and June	*53, 106*
Alyssum saxatile	Basket of Gold	S/C	3	A small plant to 8 in. (20.3 cm) with grey-green leaves covered in April and May with clouds of bright yellow flowers	41
Anaphalis margaritacea	Pearly Everlasting	SM	5	Off-white, papery, fragrant flower buttons appear on 2-ft. (61-cm) silvery-grey plants July to September	107
Anaphalis triplinervis		SM	4	Clusters of puffy white ball-like flowers on short stems	107
Anchusa azurea 'Royal Blue'	Bugloss	S/C	3	3-ft. (91.4-cm) plants with hairy, coarse leaves topped with intense true blue flower spikes June to August	38
Arctium minus	Common Burdock	T	4	Short-lived perennial with coarse leaves to 5 ft. (1.5 m) tall and hook-spined burrs in late summer and fall	118
Arrhenatherum elatius 'Variegatus'	Variegated Tall Oat Grass	S/F	3	Slender leaves to 5 ft. (1.5 m) tall with striped variegations	*60*
Artemisia abrotanum	Southernwood	SM	4	Makes shaggy, 3- to 5-ft. (91.4-cm to 1.5-m) clumps of feathery grey-green, pungently aromatic leaves	87
Artemisia absinthium	Common Wormwood	SM	4	A slightly woody evergreen artemisia with silver grey leaves 2 to 3 ft. (61 to 91.4 cm) carrying a medicinal scent	87

S=SIGHT **S/C**=SIGHT/COLOR **S/F**=SIGHT/FORM **S/L**=SIGHT/LINE **SM**=SMELL **T**=TOUCH **SO**=SOUND **TA**=TASTE **✳**=6TH SENSE

PLANT	COMMON NAME	SENSE	ZONE	DESCRIPTION	PAGE
Artemisia ludoviciana albula 'Silver King'		S/C	4	Choice silver-grey leaves 2- to 3-ft. (61 to 91.4-cm) tall carry aromatic scent	*42*, 48
Artemisia schmidtiana 'Silver Mound'		T	4	Produces round mounds of very fine, silver-grey, ornamental foliage 1 ft. (30.5 cm) high and 1½ ft. (45.7 cm) across.	118
Aruncus dioicus	Goat's Beard	S/F, T	5	A pyramid of broad, toothed leaves produces plumes of creamy white flowers in late June and July	*60*, 121
Asarum canadense	Wild Ginger	S/F	3	Grown for its shade-loving, heart-shaped low-growing foliage and its aromatic root used medicinally	*62*
Asarum europaeum		T	4	Glossy, deep-green, kidney-shaped foliage forms 6-in. (15.2-cm) ground cover in shady spots	126
Asparagus densiflorus 'Sprengeri'	Sprenger Asparagus	T	10	Needlelike leaves make 3- to 5-ft. (91.4-cm to 1.5-m) stems seem soft and fuzzy	121
Aster frikarti		SO	5	Lancelike leaves and stiff stems are topped with large lavender daisies from June to September, even longer in warm areas	*133*
Aster novae-angliae 'Harrington's Pink'	Michelmas Daisy	S	4	Profuse bloom of light pink flowers on 3- to 4-ft. (91.4-cm to 1.2-m) wiry stems in late summer, early fall	*11*
Astilbe x *arendsii* 'Fanal'		S/C	4	Bright red flowering plumes open above 2-ft. (61-cm) ferny foliage in June and July	52
Astilbe x *arendsii* 'Granat'		S/F	4	This cultivar has lighter pinkish-red flowering plumes	*60*
Athyrium filix-femina	Lady Fern	T		Vase-shaped fern to 4 ft. (1.2 m) with many feathery leaf divisions	126
Athyrium nipponicum 'Pictum' (aka *A. goeringianum* 'Pictum')	Japanese Painted Fern	T	3	Choice fern makes a small, 18-in. (45.7-cm) clump of pointed fronds with leaflets shaded from purplish through lavender to silvery grey green	126
Bergenia cordifolia	Heart-Leaved Bergenia	S/C, SM	3	Large, cabbagy leaves form 1-ft. (30.5-cm) high clumps that produce clusters of rose-pink flowers in May	37, 82–83
Brugmansia candida	Datura	SM	10	Rangy, soft green leaves to 10 or more ft. (3 m) tall with pendulous, 1-ft. (30.5-cm) long, very fragrant white trumpets spring to winter	*104*, 104–5
Campanula Formanekiana		S	4	2-ft. (61-cm) stems produce leafy panicles with clusters of white bells with main show in June	*12*
Campanula persicifolia	Peach-Leaved Bellflower	SM	3	Nodding, bright blue bells cluster along upright stems with narrow leaves from June to August	87

S=SIGHT   S/C=SIGHT/COLOR   S/F=SIGHT/FORM   S/L=SIGHT/LINE   SM=SMELL   T=TOUCH   SO=SOUND   TA=TASTE   ✳=6TH SENSE

PLANT	COMMON NAME	SENSE	ZONE	DESCRIPTION	PAGE
Campanula portenschlagiana	Dalmatian Bellflower	S/C	4	Low, 6-in. (15.2-cm) mats of toothed, heart-shaped leaves and with masses of blue-violet bells in summer	*29*
Centranthus ruber	Red Valerian	SM	5	Rich green foliage and dense clusters at end of 3-ft. (91.4-cm) branch tips produces seed that tends to self-sow in future years	85
Cerastium tomentosum	Snow-in-Summer	S/C	2	Silvery grey foliage forms a dense, 6-in. (15.2-cm) mat covered with masses of star-shaped white flowers in June	49
Cheiranthus cheiri	Wallflower	S, SM	8	Erect, bushy plants to 2 ft. (61 cm) tall produce phlox-like balls of sweet, four-petaled florets April into June	*24, 101*, 111
Chrysanthemum parthenium 'Aureum'	Golden Feverfew	S/C	6	Blooms from June to October with clusters of yellow daisy-like flowers on 2- to 3-ft. (61 to 91.4-cm) stems	52
Cimicifuga racemosa	Snakeroot	S/C, T	3	Tall wands of creamy florets spike upwards above attractive, very dark green foliage	*34, 45, 121*
Clematis				See Climbers and Vines	
Convallaria majalis	Lily-of-the-Valley	SM	2	Sweetly fragrant waxy white bells hang along nodding racemes emerging from low, ground-covering leaves	88, 98
Convolvulus mauritanicus	Ground Morning Glory	S/C	8	Mat-forming, branching, evergreen perennial with lavender blue 2-in. (5.1-cm) flowers June to November	*31, 45*
Coreopsis verticillata 'Moonbeam'		S/C, SM	4	Pale yellow starlike daisies cluster over mounds of finely filigreed foliage from July to frost	28, 43, *53*, 98
Cosmos atrosanguineus	Chocolate Cosmos	SM	8	Makes an inconspicuous clump of foliage, but chocolate daisies on long stems actually smell of chocolate	98
Crocosmia pottsii		S/C	7	A bundle of long, sword-shaped leaves produce long racemes of flaming orange red flowers in summer	43
Dennstaedtia punctilobula	Hay-Scented Fern	T	3	Small, finely-cut and dainty-looking ferns cover the ground in areas of light shade	126
Dianthus caryophyllus 'English Giants'	Carnation	S/C	6	Scarlet double carnations blossom in early summer atop sprawly 2-ft. (61-cm) stems with grey-green leaves	38
Dicentra spectabilis	Bleeding Heart	S/C, T	3	Ornate red and white heart-shaped flowers hang under gracefully arching 2-ft. (61-cm) racemes in May and June	41, 118

S=SIGHT S/C=SIGHT/COLOR S/F=SIGHT/FORM S/L=SIGHT/LINE SM=SMELL T=TOUCH SO=SOUND TA=TASTE *=6TH SENSE

PLANT	COMMON NAME	SENSE	ZONE	DESCRIPTION	PAGE
Dictamnus albus	Gas Plant	**SM**	3	Off-white, lemon-scented flowers bloom in June atop straight spikes on plants with attractive foliage	86
Equisetum hyemale	Horsetail	**T**	3	Fluted, hollow, slender stems to 3 or 4 ft. (91.4 cm or 1.2 m) are bright green and grow in dense stands in wet areas	8–9, 118
Epimedium x *rubrum*	Bishops Hat	**T**		Dainty red and yellow May-June flowers held above assymetrical tiers of heart-shaped leaves make it a choice plant	126
Eremurus 'Shelford Hybrids'	Foxtail Lily	**T**		4- to 5-ft. (1.2 to 1.5-m) tall spikes in white,buff, pink, yellow, and orange above basal rosettes of straplike leaves	121
Eschscholzia californica	California Poppy	**S/C**	4	Low-growing, finely-divided, blue-green leaves produces yellow to intense orange flowers in summer	34–35
Euphorbia characias wulfenii		**SM**	8	Upright 4-ft. (1.2-m) stems set around with slender leaves topped with masses of chartreuse flowers late winter to spring	*106*
Festuca ovina glauca	Blue Fescue	**S/C**	3	Grassy tufts with steel-blue blades grow only 8 to 10 in. (20.3 to 25.4 cm) tall	52
Filipendula ulmaria	Queen-of-the-Meadow	**T**	3	Beautiful foliage surmounted by fragrant white feathery flower plumes in June and July	*117*
Fragaria 'Baron Solemacher'	Fraises de bois	**TA**	4	A red wild European strawberry of good flavor that makes a fine edging plant in the border	142
Fragaria virginiana	Wild Strawberry	**TA**	3	This is the exquisite eastern wild strawberry that likes acid soil in old sunny fields	142
Gallium odoratum	Sweet Woodruff	**SM**	3	Thin stems have whorls of 6 to 8 slender fragrant leaves and clusters of white flowers in June and July	100
Geranium sangunieum var. *lancastriense*		**S/C**	4	Short compact plant with pure carmine pink flowers over a long season	*52*
Geranium pratense 'Johnson's Blue'		**S/C**	4	Mounds of leaves to 15 in. (38.1 cm) covered with choice blue-violet flowers in June with sparser bloom to September	*32–33*
Geranium psilostemon		**S, T**	4	A taller bushy geranium to 3 or 4 ft. (91.4 cm or 1.2 m) with showy pink-magenta flowers from June to September	*24, 117*
Geranium sanguineum	Bloody Cranesbill	**S/C**		1-ft. (30.5-cm) high mounds of finely cut foliage produce free-blooming magenta flowers from May to September	*52*

S=SIGHT **S/C**=SIGHT/COLOR **S/F**=SIGHT/FORM **S/L**=SIGHT/LINE **SM**=SMELL **T**=TOUCH **SO**=SOUND **TA**=TASTE ✳=6TH SENSE

PLANT	COMMON NAME	SENSE	ZONE	DESCRIPTION	PAGE
Gunnera manicata		S/F, S/L, T	9	Giant leaves from 4- to 8-ft. (1.2 to 2.4-m) across are held atop bristly stems to 8-ft. (2.4-m) tall for a dramatic display	65, *76*, 127
Gypsophila paniculata	Baby's Breath	S/F, T	4	Fluffy clouds of tiny white flowers float above inconspicuous grey-green foliage	65, *66*, 121
Hakonechloa macra 'Aureola'	Japanese Forest Grass	S/C	3	Looks like a small bamboo with graceful, arching 18-in. (45.7-cm) leaves of green with gold stripes	48, 52
Helianthemum nummularium	Rock Rose	S/C, S/L	5	Grey-green evergreen foliage is covered in summer with flimsy flowers in red, pink, apricot, orange, or white	*30, 74*
Helictotrichon sempervirens	Blue Oat Grass	S/C, T	3	2-ft. (61-cm) tall tufts of dusky blue, slim grass blades presist into early winter	52, 126
Heliopsis scabra 'Karat'	Hardy Zinnia	S/C	3	3- to 4-ft. (91.4-cm to 1.2-m) tall stems carry daisies from June to September	42
Helleborus foetidus	Stinking Hellebore	S/L	4	Greenish-white flowers, some with red petal tips, bloom January to March on 2-ft. (61-cm) evergreen plants	*80*
Helleborus orientalis	Lenten Rose	S/C, S/F	4	2-in. (5.1-cm) nodding flowers of white to mauve bloom March to May on 18-in. (45.7-cm) stems with evergreen leaves	48, *62*
Hemerocallis fulva	Tawny or Common Daylily	S/C	3	Orange flowers with reddish brown and yellow throats open above 3-ft. (91.4-cm) plants in late June	34, 42
Hesperis matronalis	Dame's Rocket	SM	3	Purple to white phlox-like flower clusters appear June to August on 3-ft. (91.4-cm) branching stems with toothed leaves	100
Heuchera 'Palace Purple'		TA	3	Grown for its low-growing clumps of dark reddish-purple leaves more than its flowers	147
Heuchera sanguinea	Coral Bells	S/C, S/L	3	Low clumps of evergreen leaves send up graceful stems with sprays of tiny bell-shaped coral-red flowers in May to July	*29, 75*
Hosta fortunei 'Gold Standard'		S/C	3	2-ft. (61-cm) mound of 8-in. (20.3-cm) wide ribbed seersucker leaves creamy gold edged in green	*49*
Hosta plantaginea	August Lily	SM, T	3	9-in. (22.9-cm) heart-shaped leaves form unremarkable loose clumps with richly fragrant white flowers on stalks in August	98, 100, 104, 126
Hosta sieboldiana		T	3	Blue-green, seersuckered 10- to 15-in. (25.4 to 38.1-cm) wide leaves in 2- to 3-ft. (61 to 91.4-cm) clumps	*119*

S=SIGHT S/C=SIGHT/COLOR S/F=SIGHT/FORM S/L=SIGHT/LINE SM=SMELL T=TOUCH SO=SOUND TA=TASTE ✳=6TH SENSE

PLANT	COMMON NAME	SENSE	ZONE	DESCRIPTION	PAGE
Houttuynia cordata 'Variegata'		SM	9	Low, ivy-like plant with 2- to 3-in. (5.1 to 7.6-cm) showy leaves splashed with red, yellow, pink, and cream	106
Hyssopus officinalis	Hyssop	SM	3	2-ft. (61-cm) perennial herb with narrow, dark green, anise-scented leaves and dark blue flowers in July to November	87, 107, 110
Iberis sempervirens	Candytuft	T	3	8-in. (20.3-cm) mounds of dark, glossy evergreen foliage is covered with clusters of white flowers in May and June	*117*
Iris germanica	Bearded or German Iris	S/C, SM	4	Familiar garden irises with sword-shaped leaves and flowers in every color in May and June	*32–33, 102,* 103
Iris germanica 'Florentina'	Orris Root	SM	4	The flowers are the palest blue, but the plant is known for its dried root, used in perfumes and potpourri	105
Iris pseudacorus 'Variegata'		T	5	3-ft. (91.4-cm) sword-shaped leaves and rich yellow fleur-de-lys flowers appear in June through July	*119*
Iris sibirica 'Caesar'	Siberian Iris	S/F	3	Many graceful, dark blue beardless irises appear among tips of dense, 3-ft. (91.4-cm), spiky foliage clumps	*60*
Lavandula angustifolia	English Lavender	SM	5	Grey, needlelike leaves on low stems and flower wands June to August topped with fragrant violet-blue florets	*88, 107, 110*
Lavandula dentata	French Lavender	SM	7	Narrow grey-green leaves on 3-ft. (91.4-cm) plants with lavender-purple flowers topped with a tuft of light lavender bracts	110
Lavandula stoechas	Spanish Lavender	SM	8	Much like *L. dentata*, but coarser, and of a deeper purplish color	*87, 106*
Ligularia dentata 'Othello'		*	5	Choice perennial with 1-ft. (30.5-cm) wide round leaves and orange daisy-like flowers on 3- to 4-ft. (91.4-cm to 1.2-m) stalks midsummer to fall	156
Linum perenne	Perennial Flax	S/C, T	5	Thin, 2-ft. (61-cm), graceful, arching stems with pale blue flowers opening sparsely May to August	48, *124–25*
Lobelia cardinalis	Cardinal Flower	S/C, TA	4	Basal leaf rosette sends up 3- to 4-ft. (91.4-cm to 1.2-m) spikes crowned with red tubular flowers July to September	34–35, *148*
Lobelia fulgens		S/C	7	Wild lobelia seldom seen in gardens, but a parent of the frequently-seen *L.* x *speciosa* with its intense red flowering scapes	52

S=SIGHT S/C=SIGHT/COLOR S/F=SIGHT/FORM S/L=SIGHT/LINE SM=SMELL T=TOUCH SO=SOUND TA=TASTE ✽=6TH SENSE

PLANT	COMMON NAME	SENSE	ZONE	DESCRIPTION	PAGE
Lunaria biennis	Money Plant	**SM**	4	Biennial or short-lived perennial that resembles wild mustard but with purple flowers followed by silvery disc-like pods	100
Lupinus polyphyllus	Lupine	**S/C**	4	Large racemes of pea-like flowers above pretty whorled leaves bloom June and July in many pastel colors and bicolors	*32–33*, 41
Lychnis coronaria	Rose Campion	**S/C**	3	Optically intense magenta flowers bloom in midsummer on 2-ft. (61-cm) stems with silvery grey leaves	49
Lysimachia clethroides	Gooseneck Loosestrife	**S/F**	5	3-ft. (91.4-cm), invasive plants with leafy stems and white racemes resembling goose heads in July and August	*56*
Mazus reptans		**S/L**	4	Mats of tiny leaves bear purplish-blue flowers in May and June that make *Mazus* a choice plant between stones	72
Meconopsis x *sheldonii*		**T**		A Himalayan poppy about 3- to 4-ft. (91.4-cm to 1.2-m) tall with papery blue flowers nodding at the end of long stalks	*117*
Melissa officinalis	Lemon Balm	**SM**	3	Lemony leaves of this shrubby little herb are used to flavor and scent drinks, fish dishes, sachets, and potpourri	106, 110
Mentha pulegium	Pennyroyal	**SM**	3	A small creeping plant to 6 in. (15.2 cm) tall with overly-intense mint aroma sprouts lavender flowers around stiff short stems	106
Mentha requienii	Corsican Mint	**SM**	8	Mat-forming plant with tiny light lavender flowers in summer is intensely minty when brushed	106
Miscanthus sinensis 'Gracillimus'	Maiden Grass	**T**	3	Tall, graceful fountain of narrow leaves 6- to 8-ft. (1.8 to 2.4-m) tall sports plumy seedheads in late summer	118
Miscanthus sinensis 'Variegatus'		**SO**	3	Same as *M.s.* 'Gracillimus' except that leaves are striped with white lengthwise	*133*
Monarda didyma	Bee Balm	**S/C, SM, TA**	4	Square, erect, 3-ft. (91.4-cm) stems are topped July to August with crowns of tubular red flowers surrounding a central disk	41, 98, 99, 110, 147
Monarda didyma 'Croftway Pink'		**S/C**	4	Soft pink flowers and a more compact habit characterize this choice variety of bee balm	41

S=SIGHT S/C=SIGHT/COLOR S/F=SIGHT/FORM S/L=SIGHT/LINE SM=SMELL T=TOUCH SO=SOUND TA=TASTE ✻=6TH SENSE

PLANT	COMMON NAME	SENSE	ZONE	DESCRIPTION	PAGE
Monarda fistulosa	Oswego Tea	**SM**	4	Lavender flower crowns on 3-ft. (91.4-cm) square stiffly erect stems colonize large areas where this wild species likes its spot	88, 98, 110
Nepeta faassenii (aka *Nepeta mussinii*)	Catmint	**S/C, S/F**	3	Makes 1½-ft. (45.7-cm), bushy, aromatic, grey-green plants with tiny lavender-blue flowers June to August	*32–33, 44, 49, 60*
Nicotiana alata		**SM**	5	Usually grown as an annual, this 2- to 3-ft. (61 to 91.4-cm) plant opens fragrant, tubular white flowers in early evening.	103
Nicotiana sylvestris		**SM**	5	A large, coarse, 5-ft. (1.5-m) plant with very fragrant tubular white flowers at night	103
Nierembergia hippomanica	Dwarf Cup Flower	**T**	9	Spreading low plants have 6- to 12-in. (15.2 to 30.5-cm) stems with blue-violet, bell-like cups all summer	*112–13*
Osmunda cinnamomea	Cinnamon Fern	**T**	3	2-ft. (61-cm) ferns with reddish-brown tufted fronds in center of circle of green fronds	126
Osmunda regalis 'Purpurescens'	Royal Fern	**S/F**		2- to 4-ft. (61-cm to 1.2-m) fronds with attractive stems and finely-divided, wavy-edged foliage	*60*
Pachysandra terminalis		**T**	4	Glossy, ornamental, dark evergreen leaves form ground-covering mats that spread from stoloniferous roots	126
Paeonia lactiflora	Chinese Peony	**SM**	3	Large, fragrant, round flowers appear for a short time in June on 2- to 4-ft. (61-cm to 1.2-m) densely leafy stalks	*100, 101*
Paeonia officinalis	Memorial Day Peony	**SM**	3	Old-fashioned double deep red flowers on ferny, 2-ft. (61-cm) foliage in May and June	*110*
Paeonia suffruticosa	Tree Peony	**SM**	5	Shrub to 6 ft. (1.8 m) with woody stems and very large flowers, single to double, in a wide range of colors	92, *101*
Papaver orientale 'Henfield Brilliant'	Oriental Poppy	**S/C, S/F**	3	Coarse, hairy foliage sends up long stems with orange crepe paper poppies in June	*30, 49–50, 64*
Pennisetum alopecuroides 'Hameln'	Foxtail Grass	**S, SM, T**	5	2- to 3-ft. (61 to 91.4-cm) clump of grass with foxtail-like flower heads in August and September	23, 99, 118, *122*
Pennisetum setaceum 'Cupreum'	Fountain Grass	**S/C**	4	Dense 3- to 4-ft. (91.4-cm to 1.2-m) clump of grass topped in summer with fuzzy, copper-purplish flower heads	52
Penstemon 'Evelyn'		**SM**		White to pink flowers on bushy plants	*106*

S=SIGHT S/C=SIGHT/COLOR S/F=SIGHT/FORM S/L=SIGHT/LINE SM=SMELL T=TOUCH SO=SOUND TA=TASTE ✳=6TH SENSE

PLANT	COMMON NAME	SENSE	ZONE	DESCRIPTION	PAGE
Perovskia atriplicifolia	Russian Sage	S/C	3	3-ft. (91.4-cm) bushy subshrub with fine, silvery leaves explodes into mists of tiny blue flowers in summer	41
Phlox x 'Chatahoochee'		S/F	4	Pink star-shaped flowers with red eyes appear on low-growing 8-in. (20.3-cm) stems in mid to late spring	*64*
Phlox divaricata	Wild Blue Phlox	S/C, SM	3	Small, 10-in. (25.4-cm) stems with little leaves produce clusters of lavender-blue stars in May and June	48, *91*
Phormium tenax	New Zealand Flax	S/C, S/F	8	Bold cluster of sword-like leaves up to 9 ft. (2.7 m) sometimes variegated, with exquisite coppery-pink and dwarf forms	*52, 63–65*
Platycodon grandiflorus 'Blue'	Balloon Flower	S/C, TA	3	2-ft. (61-cm) slender stems with grey-green foliage produce blue balloons that open to cups in mid-summer	28, 148
Polemonium reptans	Creeping Jacob's Ladder	S/C	3	Tufts of ferny foliage have clusters of pretty, pale blue nodding bells April to June	41, 48
Polianthes tuberosa	Tuberose	SM	11	3-ft. (91.4-cm) tuft of grasslike leaves send up slender flower stalks with loose clusters of intensely fragrant white flowers in summer and fall	103
Potentilla nepalensis 'Miss Willmott'	Cinquefoil	S/C	5	1-ft. (30.5-cm) long, low-growing branched stems with strawberry-like leaves carry smattering of carmine-rose, cup-shaped flowers from June to frost.	36
Primula alpicola	Primrose	SM, SO	4	Small clump of dark green tongue-like leaves carry clusters of white, violet, to yellow flowers on stalks in early spring	103, *135*
Rheum palmatum	Ornamental Rhubarb	S/C, S/F	3	Massive, coarsely cut leaves on long stalks with tall red flower stalk in June and July	52, *62*, 65
Rodgersia pinnata 'Superba'		S/C	6	Astilbe-like puffy bright pink flowers on tall stem in June-July held above large, palmate leaves with purple cast when young	52
Rodgersia podophylla		S	6	Showy 3-ft. (91.4-cm) foliage plant with leaves divided into large, coarsely cut leaflets and white flowers in summer	*21*
Rosmarinus officinalis	Rosemary	SM, TA	7	Woody shrub to 3 ft. (91.4 cm) tall with needlelike, aromatic leaves and tiny sprays of pale blue flowers all year	86, 87, 106, *107*, 147, 148
Rubus phoenicolasius	Wineberry	TA	5	Hairy, prickly, reddish bramble stems bear copious amounts of tart-sweet raspberry-like fruit in late July	144–46

S=SIGHT S/C=SIGHT/COLOR S/F=SIGHT/FORM S/L=SIGHT/LINE SM=SMELL T=TOUCH SO=SOUND TA=TASTE ✳=6TH SENSE

PLANT	COMMON NAME	SENSE	ZONE	DESCRIPTION	PAGE
Ruta graveolens	Rue	S/C	4	2-ft. (61-cm) bushy plant with small, round, pungent blue-green leaves, rather than inconspicuous yellow flowers, as the main feature	49
Salvia argentea	Silver Sage	S/C	4	6-in. (15.2-cm) leaves, or longer, are white with silvery hairs with flowers stems to 4 ft. (1.2 m)	49
Salvia elegans	Pineapple Sage	SM, TA	9	2- to 3-ft. (61 to 91.4-cm) plant with light green leaves used for seasoning and scarlet, edible, tubular flowers in fall	110, 147
Salvia officinalis	Garden Sage	S/C	4	Narrow, grey-green leaves used in cooking make a low mound of violet-blue flower spikes in early summer	52
Salvia x *superba*		S/L	4	Erect spikes of intense dark blue flowers on branching stems above 18-in. (45.7-cm) base of dark green leaves.	77
Santolina chamaecyparissus	Lavender Cotton	SM	6	Silver-grey, aromatic, evergreen, finely-divided leaves with yellow button flowers August-September	*107*
Santolina virens		SM	6	Dark green leaves and compact growth to 1 ft. (30.5 cm) tall with pale yellow buttonlike flowers in late summer	*107*
Saxifraga umbrosa 'Elliott's Variety'	London Pride	S/C	4	Flowers in May with loose clusters of rose-pink flowers in red stalk above rosette of small leaves	*40*
Sedum spurium 'Dragon's Blood'		S/C	4	Low-growing evergreen with trailing stems, thick, succulent bronzy leaves and rose-red flowers on short stalks in summer	52
Sedum telephium 'Autumn Joy'		T	4	Erect stems with succulent leaves 2 to 3 ft. (61 to 91.4 cm) with rosy flower heads turning copper, then burgundy, in late summer	*122*
Sedum telephium subsp. *maximum* 'Atropurpureum'		S/C	4	Oval, succulent, deep purple leaves from 18- to 24-in. (45.7 to 61-cm) tall with whitish flower heads in late summer	52
Sempervivum tectorum	Hens and Chicks	S/C, S/F	4	Compact rosettes of fleshy, evergreen leaves make offsets and short, arching stems with pink flowers in summer	49, 60
Senecio cineraria	Dusty Miller	S/C, S/F, SM	5	Showy, white, woolly leaves are cut into many lobes and makes mounds 2- to 3-ft. (61 to 91.4-cm) tall	43, 49, 63, 98
Sparaxis tricolor	Harlequin Flower	S/F	9	Short, swordlike leaves and freely produced 2-in. (5.1-cm) flowers with bold red, yellow, white, pink, or purple markings	60

S=SIGHT S/C=SIGHT/COLOR S/F=SIGHT/FORM S/L=SIGHT/LINE SM=SMELL T=TOUCH SO=SOUND TA=TASTE ✶=6TH SENSE

PLANT	COMMON NAME	SENSE	ZONE	DESCRIPTION	PAGE
Stachys byzantina	Lamb's Ears	**S, S/C, S/F, T**	4	Woolly, silver-grey leaves carpet ground to make effective contrast with green foliage plants	*24*, 49, 60, *117*, 118, *124–25*
Symphytum officinale	Comfrey	**T**	3	Straight stalks with large, coarse leaves to 3-ft. (91.4-cm) tall opening clusters of small purplish flowers in June	*127*
Tanacetum amanii	Tansy	**SM**	3	Rare species of tansy with coarse leaves and yellow, buttonlike flower heads	107
Tellima grandiflora	Fringe Cups	**T**	7	Low clumps of leaves send up 2-ft. (61-cm) flower stalks sprinkled with greenish white cups along their length	*117*
Thalictrum aquilegifolium	Columbine Meadow Rue	**S/C**	5	Airy clusters of fluffy little lavender flowers bloom in May and June above columbine-like foliage	37
Thymus citriodoris	Lemon Thyme	**SM, TA**	4	4- to 12-in. (10.2 to 30.5-cm) tall, shrubby form of thyme with lemon-scented leaves and lavender flowers in June	106, 110, 147
Thymus lanuginosis	Woolly Thyme	**T**	4	Makes a silvery-grey mat of tiny woolly leaves with rose-pink flowers in June	121
Thymus vulgaris	Common Thyme	**TA**	4	Low, 1-ft. (30.5-cm) tall woody shrubby herb with grey-green leaves and little lilac-colored flowers in June and July	150
Urtica dioica	Stinging Nettles	**T**	3	Succulent erect stems carry toothed leaves that impart a horrendous sting when touched	118
Verbascum blattaria	Moth Mullein	**T**	3	Low clumps of toothed, dark green leaves hoist 2 ½-ft. (76.2-cm) flower spikes dotted with pale yellow flowers in summer	118
Verbascum thapsus	Common Mullein	**T**	3	Common weed with fuzzy, flannel-like, large grey-green leaves that make an 18-in. (45.7-cm) rosette and send up 5-ft. (1.5-m) flower stalks with yellow flowers in summer	118
Verbena canadensis	Rose Verbena	**S**	6	Small perennial to 18 in. (45.7 cm) tall with reddish-purple blossoms over a long season	23
Veronica incana	Woolly Speedwell	**S/C, S/F**	3	Woolly, white, lacelike leaves send up slender 18-in. (45.7-cm) spikes of lavender-blue florets from June to August	49, 60
Vinca minor	Periwinkle	**S/C, T**	4	Glossy, evergreen leaves on trailing stems cover large areas, are dotted with violet-blue flowers in April and May	*48*, 126

S=SIGHT **S/C**=SIGHT/COLOR **S/F**=SIGHT/FORM **S/L**=SIGHT/LINE **SM**=SMELL **T**=TOUCH **SO**=SOUND **TA**=TASTE **✻**=6TH SENSE

PLANT	COMMON NAME	SENSE	ZONE	DESCRIPTION	PAGE
Viola odorata	Violet	**SM, TA**	5	Fragrant purple violets bloom among tufted,m heart-shaped leaves in 6-in. (15.2-cm) mounds	84, 88, 91–92, 103, 147
Viola x *wittrockiana* 'Crystal Bulb'	Pansy	**S/C**	5	Dark blue pansies bloom May to September above 6-in. (15.2-cm) clumps of light green foliage	*27*
Yucca filamentosa		**S/F**	4	4-ft. (1.2-m) sprays of large, swordlike leaves make tall flower stalk with loose, creamy-white bells in July and August	63–65

Shrubs

PLANT	COMMON NAME	SENSE	ZONE	DESCRIPTION	PAGE
Abutilon pictum 'Thompsonii'	Variegated Flowering Maple	**S/F**	9	Orange-red bells hang from long, rangy branchesin all seasons	*64*
Aloysia triphylla	Lemon Verbena	**SM**	7	A gangly shrub with lemon-scented leaves	88, 106
Azalea hybrids		**S/L**			70, 72
Brunfelsia americana	Lady of the Night	**SM**	11	Produces long, white, fragrant trumpets all year	104
Brunsfelsia pauciflora 'Floribunda'	Yesterday, Today, and Tomorrow	**SM**	8	June blooms are purple, lavender, or white if they've been open 1, 2, or 3 days	104
Buddleia alternifolia		**SM**	6	A fountain of lilac flowers on long, arching stems in June	93
Buddleia davidii	Butterfly Bush	**SM, T**	6	Fragrant lavender panicles in July	*10*, 93
Buxus sempervirens 'Suffruticosa'	True Dwarf Boxwood	**S/C, S/F**	6	Little leaves give a busy, dense texture on shrubs that grow to a maximum 5 ft. (1.5 m)	*48, 61*
Calycanthus floridus	Carolina Allspice	**SM**	4	Maroon flowers in May-June have juicy-fruit scent and brown seed pods are fragrant when crushed.	92
Camellia japonica	Camellia	**SM, T**	8	Broad-leafed evergreen shrubs with 2- to 5-in. (5.1 to 12.7-cm) white, red, rose, or pink flowers flowers in winter	93, 126
Ceanothus impressus	Santa Barbara Ceanothus	**S/C, ***	9	Myriads of tiny dark blue florets in puffy masses on evergreen shrubs in winter and early spring	*28, 158–59*
Cestrum nocturnum	Night-Blooming Jasmine	**SM**	10	Tall, rangy stems produce two or three annual flushes of small white tubes with heavy jasmine-like fragrance	87, 104, 105
Chamaecyparis obtusa 'Gracilis'	Slender Hinoki Cypress	**SO**	6	Useful, beautiful evergreen shrub grows slowly to 15 ft. (4.6 m) with very dark green foliage	*133*
Choisia ternata	Mexican Orange	**SM**	9	Produces masses of little white star-like flowers in March and April that carry orange-blossom scent	92

S=SIGHT **S/C**=SIGHT/COLOR **S/F**=SIGHT/FORM **S/L**=SIGHT/LINE **SM**=SMELL **T**=TOUCH **SO**=SOUND **TA**=TASTE *****=6TH SENSE

PLANT	COMMON NAME	SENSE	ZONE	DESCRIPTION	PAGE
Clethra alnifolia	Sweet Pepperbush	SM	3	A choice shrub or small tree to 10 ft. (3 m) with 6-in. (15.2-cm) flower spikes in late summer	93
Clethra alnifolia 'Pinkspire'		SM	3	Same as species but with pink flower spikes	93
Corylopsis pauciflora	Buttercup Winter Hazel	SM	6	Clusters of 2 or 3 bell-shaped, fragrant yellow flowers hang from bare branches in March or April	92
Corylus avellana 'Fusco-rubra'	Purple-leaved European Filbert	S/C	4	Neat shrub to 10 ft. (3 m) with roundish, purple-reddish leaves	52
Daphne burkwoodii		SM	5	Evergreen or deciduous (depending on climate) 4-ft. (1.2-m) shrub with fragrant flowers in spring and sometimes again in fall	93
Daphne cneorum	Garland Daphne	SM	4	Spreading rock-garden shrub to just 12 in. (30.5 cm) high and 3 ft. (91.4 cm) across has fragrant flowers in mid spring	92
Daphne mezereum	February Daphne	SM	4	Rangy growth to 4 ft. (1.2 m), deciduous, with fragrant clusters of reddish-purple flowers in February or March	91
Daphne odora	Winter Daphne	SM	8	A graceful, low-growing shrub with fans of evergreen leaves and intensely perfumed flowers in late winter	86, 88, 91
Deutzia gracilis	Slender Deutzia	SM	3	Gracefully arching stems 5- to 6- ft. (1.5 to 1.8-m) tall are covered with showy white flowers in May	*35*
Eleagnus angustifolia 'Coral Silver'	Russian Olive	SM, SO	3	Silvery-grey leaves on 15-ft. (4.6-m) bushy shrub produces fruit beloved of birds	49, 132
Erica carnea	Heath	T	5	Scrubby little plants grow about 1 ft. (30.5 cm) high, carry rosy-red flowers from December to June in cool, mild, oceanside climates	*114*
'Pirbright Rose'		SM		Deeper rose-red flowers than the species	*37*
'Fatsia japonica	Japanese Aralia	S/F	8	Grows 6- to 7-ft. (1.8 to 2.1-m) with large,evergreen, tropical looking leaves	65
Gardenia jasminoides	Gardenia	SM	8	Satiny, creamy-white very fragrant flowers bloom bloom sparsely on evergreen, glossy-leaved small shrub May-November	87, 93, 111
Heliotropium arborescens	Common Heliotrope	SM	9	Dark violet to white sweetly fragrant flower clusters in spring to summer	100
Hibiscus rosa-sinensis	Chinese Hibiscus	✳	9	Big 6-in. (15.2-cm) yellow flowers with cherry-red centers on rangy shrub from June to September	156

S=SIGHT   S/C=SIGHT/COLOR   S/F=SIGHT/FORM   S/L=SIGHT/LINE   SM=SMELL   T=TOUCH   SO=SOUND   TA=TASTE   ✳=6TH SENSE

PLANT	COMMON NAME	SENSE	ZONE	DESCRIPTION	PAGE
Hydrangea quercifolia	Oakleaf Hydrangea	**S/C, SM**	3	A handsome shrub with large, oak-like leaves and lacecap hydrangea flowers in summer	*34, 104*
Lantana camara 'Allgold'		**SM**	10	Vining evergreen shrub with yellow, orange, or red flowers in 2-in. (5.1-cm) clusters	*111*
Leptospermum scoparium	New Zealand Tea Tree	**S/L**	9	Tiny-leaved and angular shrub with many cultivars that burst into exquisite late winter bloom	70
Leucothoe fontanesiana	Drooping Leucothoe	**SM**	6	Arching branches 4 to 5 ft. (1.2 to 1.5 m), evergreen leaves, and drooping clusters of white flowers in spring	92
Mahonia bealei	Leatherleaf Mahonia	**SM, T**	6	Coarse, prickly leaves and very fragrant yellow bell-like flowers in March and April on 4- to 6-ft. (1.2 to 1.8-m) plants	90, 91, 126
Myrica pensylvanica	Bayberry	**S/F, SM**	7	Dark green leaves on 6- to 9-ft. (1.8 to 2.7-m) plants are fragrant with resin, berries covered with white wax used to make candles	66, 110
Opuntia bigelovii	Teddy Bear Cactus	**T**	8	2- to 8-ft. (61-cm to 2.4-m) plants with cylindrical branches and wicked spines	120
Paeonia suffruticosa	Tree Peony	**SM**	4	This woody shrub can be trained to a single trunk, has pretty leaves and branches, and 12-in. (30.5-cm) pastel flowers in May	92, *101*
Pelargonium crispum	Lemon-Scented Geranium	**SM**	9	Finely-divided leaves have lemon scent	106
Pelargonium graveolens	Rose-Scented Geranium	**SM**	9	Fine leaves smell of roses	106
Pelargonium nervosum	Lime-Scented Geranium	**SM**	9	Odor of lime given by crushed leaves	106
Pelargonium odoratissimum	Apple-Scented Geranium	**SM**	9	Crushed leaves smell of apples	106
Pelargonium tomentosum	Peppermint-Scented Geranium	**SM, T**	9	Broad leaves smell of mint	106, 118
Philadelphus coronarius	Mock Orange	**S/F, SM**	3	A Victorian favorite that grows to 8 ft. (2.4 m) and covers itself in sweetly fragrant white flowers in June	66, 92, 98
Phormium tenax	New Zealand Flax	**S/C, S/F**	8	Much like yucca except larger, to 9 ft. (2.7 m), with 5-in. (12.7-cm) wide sword-like leaves, some cultivars bronze, reddish, purple	*52*, 63–65
Photinia fraseri	Red-Leaf Photinia	**SM**	8	Rangy, multi-trunked small trees or shrubs with red new leaves that turn leathery and evergreen when mature	88
Pinus mugo mugo	Mugho Pine	**S/C, S/L**	5	Slow-growing, dense little spreading pine	28, 48, 72
Pittosporum crassifolium		**S/C**	9	Fine, grey-green leaves on medium sized bush with small maroon flowers in May and June	48

S=SIGHT S/C=SIGHT/COLOR S/F=SIGHT/FORM S/L=SIGHT/LINE SM=SMELL T=TOUCH SO=SOUND TA=TASTE ✳=6TH SENSE

PLANT	COMMON NAME	SENSE	ZONE	DESCRIPTION	PAGE
Pittosporum tobira	Japanese Pittosporum	**SM**	8	Large shrub with clusters of small, fragrant, cream-colored flowers at branch tips in spring and fall	92
Potentilla fruticosa	Bush Cinquefoil	✳	2	Pale-yellow single flowers on small, fine-leaved shrubs from June to October	156
Rhaphiolepsis indica	India Hawthorn	✳	7	White to pink 1-in. (2.5-cm) flowers form profusely at branch tips on medium shrubs from December to May	*158–59*
Ribes nigrum	Black Currant	**TA**	4	Deciduous 4-ft. (1.2-m) shrubs bear heavy June crops	142–43
Ribes odoratum	Clove Currant	**SM**	6	Spicily scented yellow flowers on 7-ft. (2.1-m) shrubs in spring	92
Ribes sanguineum	Red Flowering	**SO**	7	Showy reddish-pink flowers on 6- to 8-ft. (1.8 to 2.4-m) shrubs in spring	*137*
Rosa 'Cecile Brunner'	Climbing polyantha	**S**	6	Little pink sweetheart roses in masses	*160*
Rosa centifolia	Cabbage Rose	**SM**	6	Double pink to purple, fragrant flowers in June	109–10
Rosa damascena	Damask Rose	**SM**	6	Pink to deep rose, fragrant, very double roses	12, 88, 110
Rosa damascena 'Ispahan'		**SM**	6	Light pink, very fragrant rose blooms over long season	88
Rosa damascena 'Mme. Hardy'		**SM**	6	Highly rated, strongly-scented white roses	88
Rosa 'Friendship'		**SM**	6		*109*
Rosa 'Fru Dagmar Hartopp'	Rugosa	**TA**	6	Single, scented, clear pink flowers all year	*143*
Rosa 'Fruhlingsgold'	Hybrid spinospissima	**S/C**	7	Light yellow almost single roses	*30*
Rosa gallica	French Rose	**SM**	6	Rose-red to pink, highly scented shrubby roses	88, 110
Rosa 'Gruss an Aachen'	Floribunda	**SM**	6	Light shell-pink rose with fruity scent	12
Rosa moschata	Musk rose	**SM**	5	The species opens cream then turns white in summer	88
Rosa 'Nevada'	Hybrid moyesii	**S**	6	Slightly double white roses with yellow centers	*24*
Rosa 'Queen Elizabeth'	Grandiflora	**SM**	5	Highly rated gorgeous pink roses	88
Rosa 'Ramona'	Hybrid laevigata	✳	5	Deep pink single roses on large shrubs	*158–59*
Rosa 'The Fairy'	Polyantha	**S/F**	6	Profuse bloom of little pink flowers in June	66
Rosmarinus officinalis	Rosemary	**SM, TA**	8	Vigorous, drought-resistant, woody-stemmed herb with medicinal smell and many clear blue flowers	86, 87, 106, 107, 147, 148

S=SIGHT **S/C**=SIGHT/COLOR **S/F**=SIGHT/FORM **S/L**=SIGHT/LINE **SM**=SMELL **T**=TOUCH **SO**=SOUND **TA**=TASTE ✳=6TH SENSE

PLANT	COMMON NAME	SENSE	ZONE	DESCRIPTION	PAGE
Sambucus canadensis	Elderberry	**T, TA**	4	6- to 7-ft. (1.8 to 2.1-m) shrub with white flower clusters in spring and edible blue-black berries in summer	118, 146, 148
Sarcococca humilis	Sarcococca	**SM**	5	Shade-loving, low-growing shrub to 18 in. (45.7 cm)	91
Syringa chinensis	Chinese lilac	**SM**	3	Large panicles of lilac florets on slender arching branches in May	92
Syringa vulgaris	Common Lilac	**SM**		Tall multi-stemmed shrubs with fragrant panicles of lilac florets in May	88, 92
Taxus baccata 'adpressas'	English Yew	**S/F**	7	Wide-spreading, dense, dark green, evergreen shrub to 5 ft. (1.5 m)	66
Viburnum burkwoodii		**SM**	3	Fragrant white blooms in spring on 6- to 10-ft. (1.8 to 3-m) deciduous shrubs	92
Viburnum carlecephalum	Fragrant Snowball	**SM**	3	10-ft. (3-m) deciduous shrub with fragrant white flowerballs in late spring to early summer	92
Viburnum carlesii	Korean Spice Viburnum	**SM**	3	Compact deciduous shrub to 6 ft. (1.8 m) with pink flowers prized for their sweet, intense fragrance	12, 87, 92
Viburnum fragrans		**SM**	4	7-ft. (2.1-m) shrub with sparse but highly fragrant flowers	91
Viburnum juddii		**SM**	6	Similar to *V. carlesii* but a bit more spreading	92
Viburnum macrocephalum	Chinese Snowball	**S/C**	3	Large deciduous shrub to 18 ft. (5.5 m) with white flower balls in April and May	*35*
Viburnum plicatum tomentosum	Japanese Snowball	**SM**		White flowerballs cluster in rows along horizontal branches of deciduous shrub reaching 15 ft. (4.6 m)	92
Weigela hybrida 'Looymansia Aurea'		**S/C**	4	A deciduous shrub that's a trouble-free and reliable bloomer in the May-June border	*44*

Trees

PLANT	COMMON NAME	SENSE	ZONE	DESCRIPTION	PAGE
Abies balsamea	Balsam Fir	**SM**	4	Dark conical shape	106
Acer japonicum 'Aureum'	Golden Fullmoon Maple	**S/C**	4	Golden foliage	52
Acer negundo 'Variegatum'	Variegated Box Elder	**S/C**	4	Variegated foliage	52
Acer palmatum	Japanese Maple	**S, S/C**	4	Elegant shape	*23, 30,* 52
Acer palmatum var. *dissectum*	Laceleaf Japanese Maple	**S/L**	4	Lacy foliage	72
Aesculus hippocastanum	Horse Chestnut	**S/C, T**	5	Upright white candles in May	36, 120
Amelanchier canadensis	Serviceberry	**S/L**	4	Drooping white clusters April	70
Arbutus menziesii	Madrone	**S/L**	7	Broad-leafed evergreen beautiful in every season	*69*

S=SIGHT **S/C**=SIGHT/COLOR **S/F**=SIGHT/FORM **S/L**=SIGHT/LINE **SM**=SMELL **T**=TOUCH **SO**=SOUND **TA**=TASTE ✳=6TH SENSE

PLANT	COMMON NAME	SENSE	ZONE	DESCRIPTION	PAGE
Betula alleghaniensis	Yellow Birch	T	5	Silvery, papery bark	118
Betula lenta	Black Birch	SM	5	Black bark with wintergreen aroma	105
Betula nigra	River Birch	T	3	Exfoliating, papery bark	*115*
Betula pendula	European Birch	T	5	Multi-trunked, arching white birches	123
Carya ovata	Hickory	T	5	Stately tree with shaggy bark, good nuts	120
Cedrus deodara 'White Imp'		T	5	Soft-looking, with downward sweeping branches	*121*
Cedrus libani	Cedar of Lebanon	T	7	Neat tufts of needles, large form	126
Chamaecyparus lawsoniana	Lawson Cypress	S/C	8	Elegant evergreen	49
Cladrastis lutea	Yellowwood	S/C, SM	3	Hanging white fragrant flower clusters June	36–37, 90–91
Cornus florida	Flowering Dogwood	S/L, T, SO	5	Large white flowers decorate small trees in April and May	70, 126, 132
Cornus mas	Cornelian Cherry	TA	5	Yellow flower clusters in March	146
Corylus americana	American hazlenut	T	5	Good understory filler	120
Corylus avellana 'Fusco-Rubra'	European Filbert	S/C	5	Purple leaves	52
Corylus maxima 'Purpurea'	Purple Filbert	S/C		Dark purple leaves	52
Cotinus coggygria 'Purpureus'	Purple Smoke Tree	S/C, S/F, S/L	5	Cloudlike flower puffs in pinkish-lavender in July and August	52, *60*, 70
Crataegus laevigata	English Hawthorn	SM	4	Red berries much of the winter	*84*, 88
Eucalyptus spp.	Eucalyptus	S/C, SM	9	Many species vary widely in size, form	52, 106
Fagus grandifolia	American Beech	T	4	Beautiful form, smooth gray bark	118
Fagus sylvatica	European Beech	S/C	4	Beautiful form, bark, twigs, leaves	52
Fagus sylvatica 'Tricolor'		S/C	4	Leaves green, white, and pink	52
Franklinia alatamaha	Franklin Tree	SM	5	Broad white cups in August, September	91
Hamamelis x *intermedia* 'Ruby Glow'	Witch Hazel	S	7	Coppery-red flowers December to March, good fall foliage color.	*22*
Hamamelis mollis	Chinese Witch Hazel	SM	7	Fragrant yellow and red flowers December-March	90
Hamamelis virginiana	Common Witch Hazel	SM	5	Yellow flowers November-December	90
Juglans nigra	Black Walnut	T	6	Large tree with excellent nuts	120
Juniperus occidentalis	Western Juniper	S/C	3	Beautiful blue-gray foliage	49
Juniperus virginiana 'Skyrocket'		S/F	3	Tall and narrow blue-gray spike	66
Koelreuteria paniculata	Golden-Rain Tree	SM	5	Yellow flower clusters in July	91
Lagerstroemia indica	Crape Myrtle	S/F	7	Clusters of red, pink, lavender or white flowers July to September	66

S=SIGHT S/C=SIGHT/COLOR S/F=SIGHT/FORM S/L=SIGHT/LINE SM=SMELL T=TOUCH SO=SOUND TA=TASTE ✳=6TH SENSE

PLANT	COMMON NAME	SENSE	ZONE	DESCRIPTION	PAGE
Magnolia grandiflora	Southern Magnolia	**SM, T**	7	Large, fragrant, waxy white flowers April to August	88, 90, 118, 126
Magnolia quinquepeta 'Nigra'	Lily Magnolia	**S**	6	Lily-like flowers are dark purple outside and pink inside, with long bloom time in spring to summer.	*21*
Magnolia heptapeta	Yulan Magnolia	**SM**	5	Very fragrant, bowl-shaped white flowers April	90
Magnolia soulangiana	Saucer Magnolia	**S/L**	5	Flowers white with mauve tinge in April	70
Magnolia stellata	Star Magnolia	**SM**	4	3-in. (7.6-cm) starlike, fragrant flowers in April	90
Oxydendron arboreum	Sourwood	**SM**	7	Fragrant white panicles of bell-shaped florets in June	90
Picea pungens	Colorado Spruce	**S, S/C**	4	Some varieties have blue-gray needles 'Montgomery' has very blue needles	*23*, 49
Pseudotsuga menziesii	Douglas Fir	**SO**	2	Stately conifer characteristic of Pacific Northwest	*137*
Prunus cerasifera	Myrobalan Plum	**S/C**	4	White flowers mass on bare branches in April	52
Prunus persica 'Frost'	Peach	**TA**	7	Excellent variety; needs winter chilling	*141*, 144
Prunus subhirtella 'Pendula'	Weeping Cherry	**S/L**	4	A fountain of pink flowers in April	*71*
Prunus tomentosa	Nanking Cherry	**SM, TA**	4	White flowers in spring	92, 146
Pterostyrax hispidus	Epaulette Tree	**SM**	5	Fragrant white tufts form panicles in June	90
Pyrus salicifolia 'Pendula'	Weeping Willow-Leafed Pear	**S/C**	5	Beautiful pendant form	*40*
Quercus garryana	Oregon White Oak	**S/L**	7	Large oak with twisty branches, grey bark	*81*
Robinia pseudoacacia 'Frisia'	Black Locust	**S/C**	3	Rose, pea-like flowers hang in clusters in May-June.	52, *60*
Salix alba tristis	Golden Weeping Willow	**S/F**	4	Year-old twigs are bright yellow	*60*
Sassafras albidum	Sassafras	**SM**	5	Small weedy trees with great fall color	105, 110
Sorbus aucuparia	European Mountain Ash	**TA**	3	Compact tree with orange-red berries in regular clusters that hang through fall	*145*
Styrax obassia	Japanese Snowbell	**SM**	6	Small white fragrant flowers in 4-in. (10.2-cm) racemes in June	90
Taxus baccata	English Yew	**S/C, S/F, S/L, SM**	5	Dark-needled slow grower eventually reachs 30 ft. (9.1 m)	49, 52, *61*, 66, 72, 89
Thuja plicata 'Aurea'	Western Red Cedar	**S/C, S/F**	4	Branch tips golden-green	52, 66
Thuja occidentalis 'Rheingold'	American Arborvitae	**S/C**	6	Golden foliage color	52

S=SIGHT S/C=SIGHT/COLOR S/F=SIGHT/FORM S/L=SIGHT/LINE SM=SMELL T=TOUCH SO=SOUND TA=TASTE *=6TH SENSE

AVERAGE WORLD CLIMATE

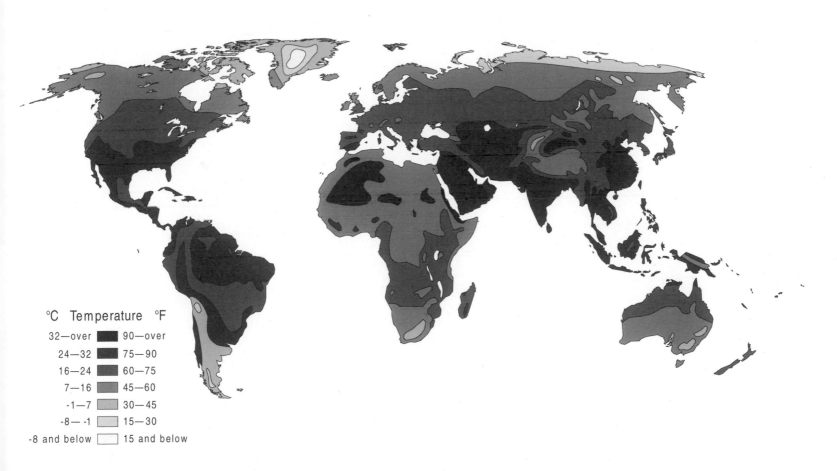

°C Temperature °F

32—over	90—over
24—32	75—90
16—24	60—75
7—16	45—60
-1—7	30—45
-8— -1	15—30
-8 and below	15 and below

UNITED STATES DEPARTMENT OF AGRICULTURE
PLANT HARDINESS ZONE MAP

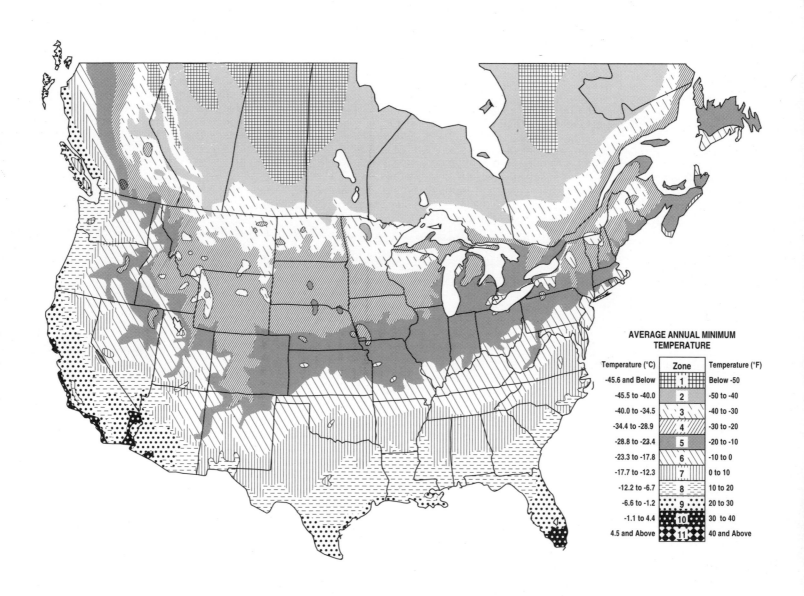

AVERAGE ANNUAL MINIMUM TEMPERATURE

Temperature (°C)	Zone	Temperature (°F)
-45.6 and Below	1	Below -50
-45.5 to -40.0	2	-50 to -40
-40.0 to -34.5	3	-40 to -30
-34.4 to -28.9	4	-30 to -20
-28.8 to -23.4	5	-20 to -10
-23.3 to -17.8	6	-10 to 0
-17.7 to -12.3	7	0 to 10
-12.2 to -6.7	8	10 to 20
-6.6 to -1.2	9	20 to 30
-1.1 to 4.4	10	30 to 40
4.5 and Above	11	40 and Above

INDEX

(Page numbers in *italic* refer to illustrations.)